ALEXI KAYE CAMPBELL

The Pride premiered at the Royal Court Theatre in London in November 2008, and received the Critics' Circle Award for Most Promising Playwright. The production was also awarded the Laurence Olivier Award for Outstanding Achievement in an Affiliate Theatre. The play received its American premiere at the Lucille Lortel Theatre, New York, in 2010. His other plays include *Apologia* (Bush Theatre, London, 2009), and *The Faith Machine* (Royal Court, London, 2011). As an actor, Alexi's work includes seasons at the Royal Shakespeare Company and productions at the Royal Court, Lyric Hammersmith, Chichester Festival Theatre, Manchester Royal Exchange, Oxford Stage Company and with Shared Experience.

Other Titles from Nick Hern Books

Alexi Kaye Campbell

THE PRIDE

NICK HERN BOOKS
London
www.nickhernbooks.co.uk

A Nick Hern Book

The Pride first published in Great Britain as a paperback original in 2008 by Nick Hern Books Limited, 14 Larden Road, London W3 7ST, in association with the Royal Court Theatre, London

Reprinted with revisions 2009, 2010, 2011

The Pride copyright © 2008, 2009 Alexi Kaye Campbell

Alexi Kaye Campbell has asserted his right to be identified as the author of this work

Cover illustration by Josie Jammet
Cover designed by Ned Hoste, 2H

Typeset by Nick Hern Books, London
Printed in the UK by CLE Print Ltd, St Ives, Cambs PE27 3LE

A CIP catalogue record for this book is available from the British Library

ISBN   978 1 84842 019 9

The Pride was first performed at the Jerwood Theatre Upstairs at the Royal Court Theatre, London, on 21 November 2008, with the following cast:

PHILIP   JJ Feild
OLIVER   Bertie Carvel
SYLVIA   Lyndsey Marshal
THE MAN / PETER /   Tim Steed
THE DOCTOR

Director   Jamie Lloyd
Designer   Soutra Gilmour
Lighting Designer   Jon Clark
Music and Sound Designers   Ben and Max Ringham

The Pride received its American premiere at the Lucille Lortel Theatre, produced by MCC Theater, on 27 January 2010, with the following cast:

PHILIP   Hugh Dancy
OLIVER   Ben Whishaw
SYLVIA   Andrea Riseborough
THE MAN / PETER /   Adam James
THE DOCTOR

Director   Joe Mantello
Designer   David Zinn
Lighting Designer   Paul Gallo
Sound Designer   Jill B.C. DuBoff

To my parents, with love

Author's Note

The main challenge in any production of this play is to handle effectively the constant scene and costume changes between the two different eras it is set in. How the director and designer deal with this challenge is up to them. Here, though, are a couple of thoughts.

When the play begins we should feel as if we are watching a 1950's drawing-room play. Only as the play progresses does this world slowly start to disintegrate and break up. The furniture and walls gradually disappear until we find ourselves in the multi-locational second half. Then, the settings become less illustrative and more suggestive. A park bench signifies a park, a sofa signifies Sylvia's flat.

One idea is to make a virtue of the costume changes – perhaps they take place somewhere on stage and are partly visible to the audience. Something more stylised. This might help the transitions between scenes become easier and more fluid.

The most important quality is one of confluence. The two different periods should meld into each other. They are distinct from each other in appearance but they know each other in spirit: a young woman standing next to her elder self. Different clothes, different hairstyles, different textures of skin... but the eyes are the same. The past is a ghost in the present just as the present is a ghost of prescience in the past.

Thanks to Ruth Little, Polly Teale, Nick Hytner, Federay Holmes, John Sackville, Noa Maxwell, Mark Leadbetter, Stephen Omer, Victoria Hamilton, Ben Daniels, Gregor Truter, and everyone at the National Theatre Studio.

Characters

1958
OLIVER, *mid-thirties*
PHILIP, *mid-thirties*
SYLVIA, *mid-thirties*
THE DOCTOR, *late thirties*

2008
OLIVER, *mid-thirties*
PHILIP, *mid-thirties*
SYLVIA, *mid-thirties*
THE MAN
PETER

OLIVER, PHILIP *and* SYLVIA *are to be played by the same actors in both periods. One actor plays the* DOCTOR, *the* MAN *and* PETER.

ACT ONE

1958

PHILIP *and* SYLVIA*'s apartment in London. It is modest but tasteful. Lots of books, a sofa and armchairs, a few pictures on the wall.*

PHILIP *is standing by the front door. He is dressed for a night out.* OLIVER *has just arrived.*

OLIVER. Philip.

PHILIP. Oliver.

OLIVER. Yes.

PHILIP. At last.

OLIVER. Yes.

PHILIP. I've heard so many things.

OLIVER. Have you?

PHILIP. So many things about you.

OLIVER. Gosh.

PHILIP. All good.

OLIVER. That's a relief.

PHILIP. Sylvia's always talking about you.

OLIVER. Is she?

PHILIP. I'm beginning to get rather jealous.

OLIVER. No need, I'm sure.

PHILIP. She thinks you're a genius.

OLIVER. There are many things I am, but a genius is definitely not one of them.

PHILIP. Extraordinary is what she calls you.

OLIVER. Does she?

PHILIP. Out of the ordinary.

A slight pause.

Let me take your coat.

OLIVER. Thank you.

OLIVER *takes off his coat and hands it to* PHILIP, *who hangs it up carefully.*

PHILIP. I'm afraid the lady is running a little late. Applying the face paint, I believe. That ancient ritual.

OLIVER. I'm early.

PHILIP. Not at all. You're right on time.

OLIVER. I walked. I thought it would take me slightly longer.

PHILIP. It's a lovely evening.

OLIVER. Well, no rain in any case.

PHILIP. All the way from Maida Vale?

OLIVER. Yes, Maida Vale.

PHILIP. Across the park, eh?

OLIVER. Yes.

PHILIP. That's a long walk.

OLIVER. I enjoyed it.

PHILIP. It's the season for it.

OLIVER. Everything in full bloom.

PHILIP. Lovely.

A slight pause.

What can I get you to drink?

OLIVER. A Scotch?

PHILIP. Ice and water?

OLIVER. Perfect.

PHILIP. I think I'll have the same.

> PHILIP *walks over to a small drinks table and pours them a couple of drinks.*

> She thinks your stories are wonderful.

OLIVER. She's certainly captured the spirit of the thing.

PHILIP. She seems to care. About the book, I mean.

OLIVER. She's very, very talented.

PHILIP. Can't stop talking about it. Something about a garden.

OLIVER. Well, it's more of a jungle, really.

PHILIP. A jungle.

OLIVER. Let's call it a jungle in the heart of England. Or at least a very overgrown and rather tropical garden.

PHILIP. What is it with children's writers and gardens? There seems to be a proliferation of them. Most of them secret, I dare say.

OLIVER. You're right.

PHILIP. Well, she's very busy with it in any case. Sketches of strange creatures all over the place. I came across a rather alarming picture of something that resembled a two-headed antelope in the bathroom the other day. Fascinating.

OLIVER. That'll be the Bellyfinch. I'm supposed to be having a first look at it on Friday morning, I believe.

PHILIP. Bellyfinch indeed. I'm afraid by comparison my life seems rather lacklustre.

OLIVER. I don't honestly believe there is such a thing as a lacklustre life.

PHILIP. You haven't sold property for a living.

OLIVER. Unexplored perhaps, but not lacklustre.

PHILIP *hands him his drink. They sit.*

PHILIP. I've never met anyone like you before. A writer, I mean.

OLIVER. Haven't you?

PHILIP. Apart from this ghastly friend of my mother's who's published a book on baking cakes.

OLIVER. Baking cakes?

PHILIP. I'm not sure that really counts.

OLIVER. That sounds a little unfair. Nothing wrong with books about cakes.

PHILIP. Have you only ever written for children?

OLIVER. For the most part. But I've written two travel books as well.

PHILIP. Sylvia mentioned it. One on Athens.

OLIVER. I lived there for a year.

PHILIP. And the other?

OLIVER. The other on the Lebanon.

PHILIP. The Lebanon?

OLIVER. But mostly I'm drawn to writing for children.

PHILIP. I wonder why.

OLIVER. I don't really know. I think it might have something to do with running completely wild.

PHILIP. Wild?

OLIVER. The possibilities are infinite. The parameters and conventions of adult fiction I find a great deal more restrictive.

PHILIP. I see.

OLIVER. I feel a lot happier in a world of talking tigers and magic mirrors. More in my element, really.

PHILIP. Fair enough.

OLIVER. Maybe one day adult fiction will embrace my more extravagant flights of fancy, but for the time being I'm quite happy writing for the under-twelves.

PHILIP. Well, it seems to keep a roof over your head.

OLIVER. A leaking one, but yes, just about.

PHILIP. Well, here's to the book anyway.

OLIVER. The book.

They toast.

PHILIP. It's strange.

OLIVER. What is?

PHILIP. When I opened the door.

OLIVER. Yes?

PHILIP. You look familiar, is what I think I'm saying.

OLIVER. Yes, I thought so too.

PHILIP. Did you?

OLIVER. Yes, I think I did.

PHILIP. Well, maybe we've bumped into each other. On the Underground or something.

OLIVER. Maybe.

PHILIP. Stranger things have happened.

Pause.

Or maybe it's just because she talks about you so often.

OLIVER. Talks about me?

PHILIP. So perhaps that's why I felt like I'd seen you before.

OLIVER. How d'you mean?

PHILIP. Oh, it's just that sometimes if you've heard a great deal about someone, if you've been expecting them in some way, you sort of imagine them before they actually arrive.

OLIVER. Yes.

PHILIP. If you know what I mean.

OLIVER. Yes, I think I do.

SYLVIA enters. She is smartly dressed for an evening out.

PHILIP. Here she is.

SYLVIA (*to* OLIVER). Has he been interrogating you?

PHILIP. Mercilessly.

OLIVER. Hello, Sylvia.

SYLVIA. He's a very jealous kind of man.

PHILIP. Rabid with it.

SYLVIA. Can easily become violent. Philip, be a darling and do me up.

She turns her back to him so that he can help her with the top hook of her dress.

Comes in handy though from time to time, I must say. I see he's offered you a drink.

OLIVER. He's been the perfect host.

SYLVIA. So all that training wasn't a complete waste of time after all.

PHILIP. I'm learning fast. Gin?

SYLVIA. I've booked the table for eight.

PHILIP. A quick one.

SYLVIA. Thank you, darling.

PHILIP goes to the bar to pour her a drink.

PHILIP. I've been telling Oliver how you keep talking about him.

SYLVIA. You haven't been embarrassing me in front of my employer, have you?

PHILIP. Probably.

SYLVIA. I've been rather nervous, you know. God knows why.

OLIVER. Nervous?

SYLVIA. About the two of you meeting.

PHILIP. She has been putting it off, hasn't she, Oliver?

OLIVER. Now that you mention it.

SYLVIA. It's a silly thing, really. I suppose it's just that I want
you to get on.

PHILIP. We were doing just fine.

SYLVIA. To like each other, I mean.

OLIVER. I don't see why we shouldn't.

PHILIP. As long as I don't discover you've been having a torrid
affair behind my back we should get on just fine.

SYLVIA. I did warn you about his sense of humour, Oliver.

PHILIP. Sense of humour?

SYLVIA. Or lack of it, I should say.

PHILIP. You're heartless.

SYLVIA. Just honest.

   A slightly awkward pause. PHILIP *hands* SYLVIA *her drink.*

   I hope you like Italian food, Oliver.

PHILIP. We've made a reservation at a little Italian place
around the corner.

OLIVER. Lovely.

SYLVIA. Philip's always making fun of it but I find it charming.

PHILIP. It's extremely red. Everything in it is red.

OLIVER. I'm partial to a little red.

PHILIP. The walls, the tablecloths, the waiter's face.
Everything's red.

SYLVIA. Philip's convinced they're not real Italians.

PHILIP. They're Yugoslavians. I'm convinced they're Yugoslavians pretending to be Italians.

OLIVER. It sounds interesting.

SYLVIA. But the food is good.

PHILIP. With a strong Serbian flavour to it.

OLIVER. Delicious, I'm sure.

A slight pause as they all sit down.

I'm very pleased to hear that a Bellyfinch has been spotted hanging around the house.

SYLVIA. Just a preliminary sketch, I'm afraid, but it's getting there.

OLIVER. I can't wait to see it.

SYLVIA. Hopefully by Friday it will be a little more confident. As we speak it's looking a trifle too purple for its own good.

PHILIP. All this talk of Bellyfinch and Hampshire jungles has made me very curious. I can't wait to read the damn thing.

SYLVIA. Well, you'll have to be patient, won't you?

OLIVER. Nearly there.

SYLVIA. Nearly. And in the meantime, you're not to snoop.

PHILIP. It's not my fault if you leave pictures of alarming things scattered across our home.

OLIVER. Is he a snooper?

SYLVIA. Of the very worst kind.

PHILIP. In the bathroom. On the sofa. Even in the fridge.

OLIVER. The fridge?

SYLVIA. Just once.

PHILIP. Something brown crawling up a tree. In the fridge. It was most disconcerting.

SYLVIA. The doorbell was ringing. I was preparing dinner. A moment of absent-mindedness, that's all.

PHILIP. Your story has invaded us. And then I'm accused of being a snooper.

OLIVER. Please accept my apologies.

PHILIP. Apologies accepted.

They laugh. There is a pause.

I am envious of you two, you know.

OLIVER. Envious?

SYLVIA. Whatever of?

PHILIP. Oh, you know, your work. Doing something creative I suppose is what I mean. Being able to invest a certain amount of passion in what you do for a living.

OLIVER. It doesn't feel passionate. Lonely more like.

SYLVIA. Philip is very frustrated in his work, aren't you, darling?

PHILIP. I sell houses, Oliver.

OLIVER. You were saying.

PHILIP. Houses and flats.

SYLVIA. The thing that you really ought to know is that Philip came into his line of work almost by accident.

OLIVER. Accident?

PHILIP. My father died.

SYLVIA. Philip's father died when he was just twenty-one.

PHILIP. I'd just left university.

SYLVIA. Philip's father had spent years running his own business buying and selling property. Philip's brother was all set up to take it over.

PHILIP. Well, he was being groomed for it, really. Father was grooming him for it. I was the useless one. Rather aimless, I'm afraid.

SYLVIA. But then two years later, Roger –

PHILIP. That's my brother.

SYLVIA. Roger was killed.

PHILIP. It was an accident.

SYLVIA. A car accident. A terrible thing.

PHILIP. I had to look after my mother.

SYLVIA. And your sister.

PHILIP. So I had no choice, really. The business just sort of fell into my hands, as it were.

SYLVIA. I sometimes wonder what you would have done. What you would have been. If things had turned out differently, I mean.

PHILIP. God knows, so do I. I'd have emigrated, probably.

OLIVER. Emigrated?

SYLVIA. Philip's always had this terribly mad idea of emigrating.

OLIVER. How exciting.

SYLVIA. Australia, Canada, that sort of thing.

PHILIP. Somewhere new.

SYLVIA. Do you remember you became obsessed with the whole idea of moving to Africa?

PHILIP. Africa, yes.

SYLVIA. He read every possible book that he could get his hands on. Books on Kenya, books on Rhodesia. They were strewn all over the house.

OLIVER. I'd love to visit Africa.

PHILIP. Never did make it further than Brighton, I'm afraid.

SYLVIA. One day.

OLIVER. One day.

PHILIP. Then next thing you know you wake up and you've spent the good part of your life showing people around empty flats.

SYLVIA. There are worse things one could do with one's life.

PHILIP. Are there?

OLIVER. I'm sure Sylvia's right.

PHILIP (*kindly*). She always is.

Pause.

Now you on the other hand, Oliver, have made it beyond Brighton.

OLIVER. I've been to a few places.

SYLVIA. Oh, stop being modest, you've been absolutely everywhere.

OLIVER. Not quite everywhere.

SYLVIA. Oliver lived in Greece.

PHILIP. Yes, he was saying…

SYLVIA. And Italy. And Beirut. And Syria.

OLIVER. I do have an affinity with that part of the world.

PHILIP. How exciting. To have lived there.

SYLVIA. Oliver was based in Athens.

PHILIP. How wonderful.

OLIVER. I lived in a tiny little house at the foot of the Acropolis. Infested with mice, but absolutely charming.

SYLVIA. How utterly romantic.

OLIVER. If you craned your neck outside the kitchen window you could just about catch a glimpse of the Parthenon.

PHILIP. The Parthenon.

SYLVIA. Philip and I are determined to drive down to Greece one day, aren't we, darling?

PHILIP. If you say so.

SYLVIA. Down through France and Italy and across the Adriatic.

PHILIP. One day.

SYLVIA. And then on to the islands.

OLIVER. The islands are beautiful.

SYLVIA. Philip, myself, a couple of copies of *The Odyssey* and a chessboard.

PHILIP. Not forgetting the gin, of course.

OLIVER. Not forgetting the gin.

SYLVIA. One day.

There is a pause. Suddenly, SYLVIA *remembers something. She turns to* OLIVER.

Tell him about Delphi.

PHILIP. Delphi?

SYLVIA. Yes, Delphi. The story about what happened to you in Delphi.

OLIVER. Oh, that…

SYLVIA. Your epiphany in Delphi.

PHILIP. What epiphany in Delphi?

SYLVIA. Oliver told me a wonderful story…

OLIVER. It's nothing really.

PHILIP. An epiphany in Delphi.

SYLVIA. It's wonderful.

PHILIP. Sounds like the title of a dreadful novel. *An Epiphany in Delphi.*

OLIVER. I don't know whether Philip…

SYLVIA. We took a break from work the other day and Oliver told me he'd been to Delphi.

OLIVER. It's not much of a story. Maybe some other time.

SYLVIA. And that something had happened to him there. Is it fair to call it a mystical experience?

PHILIP. Oh, you must say.

OLIVER. I really don't think...

PHILIP. Please.

OLIVER. It's not really that exciting or interesting. In a matter of fact it's not much of a story at all. It was just this funny thing that happened.

PHILIP. I'm all ears.

OLIVER. You'll be very disappointed, I'm afraid.

SYLVIA. Oh, go on, Oliver.

OLIVER. Well, I'd gone up to Delphi because it was one of the places in Greece, one of the sites I most wanted to visit.

SYLVIA. The oracle.

OLIVER. So I'd taken this rickety old bus from Athens and it took hours and hours and it twisted its way through the mountain roads and I remember we arrived just before the sun was going down and it dropped us off just outside this little hotel. The Hotel Zeus or something. And there were a few other foreigners – an old American couple and a German and a few other English people including this insufferable woman with a loud pompous voice and very confident opinions.

PHILIP. Not the most winning combination.

OLIVER. And we all had a bite for dinner and then went straight to sleep.

PHILIP. I'm riveted already.

OLIVER. And the next morning I woke up and opened the shutters and, well... the view was absolutely...

SYLVIA. Breathtaking.

OLIVER. The view was absolutely breathtaking. I mean, I can't do it justice. I can't attempt to describe it. You'd have to go and see it for yourself. To believe it.

PHILIP. One day.

OLIVER. The landscape, you see, the position of it. It is quite mesmerising. Very, very dramatic. Because you are high up in the mountains and on the peaks above us there was even snow, but then you look down, down through these silver slanting olive groves and you can see the sea.

SYLVIA. How beautiful.

OLIVER. You can see the waters of the Corinthian Gulf. So there is something very spectacular. I mean, truly, truly beautiful. And you begin to realise why it is that the Greeks chose that place for their oracle. That maybe in a place of such beauty and stillness you could have a sense of things to come. It takes you out of your time, out of time. You could see the bigger picture in a way.

PHILIP. Is that it? Your epiphany?

OLIVER. I've barely started.

SYLVIA. Oh, Philip, give the man a chance.

OLIVER. So after breakfast I set off towards the ancient theatre and the site of the oracle and I had the old Americans in tow. I think they thought I was a classics scholar or something. They kept asking me these questions and were very disappointed when my answers weren't quite as thorough as they were expecting.

SYLVIA. You do look the part. Especially when you're wearing your specs.

OLIVER. Well, eventually I succeeded in shrugging them off. I lost them somewhere and was able to continue on my own. Which was rather a relief, I must say.

PHILIP. I'm not surprised. One does not want to have a spiritual experience with American tourists in close proximity.

OLIVER. I just started wandering around the site. I was completely on my own and it was very, very quiet. All you could hear was the incessant humming of the cicadas. And a bit of a breeze playing through the trees. And I just walked through the place in a bit of a daze, really.

PHILIP. I feel an epiphany coming.

OLIVER. And then I heard it.

PHILIP. Told you.

OLIVER. I suppose I can only describe it as a voice. Not a voice in any conventional sense. Not the kind of voice one could immediately identify as in any way recognisable.

PHILIP. Are you sure it wasn't one of the Americans?

SYLVIA. Oh, Philip, do be quiet.

PHILIP. Pearls before swine.

OLIVER. I just stood there and I heard this voice. And it pretty much said that everything was going to be all right.

PHILIP. All right? What was going to be all right?

OLIVER. Well, that one day, maybe many, many years from now, there will be an understanding of certain things, a deeper understanding of certain aspects of our natures that would make all the difficulties we now feel, all the fears we now hold onto and the sleepless nights we now have seem almost worthwhile... And that the people who live in those times, be it fifty or five hundred years from now will be happy with that understanding and wiser for it. Better.

SYLVIA. How wonderfully Chekhovian.

OLIVER. And it sort of felt that this voice was coming to me in some way from that very future. Some future awareness of ourselves as it were. And that's it, really. That was my epiphany.

SYLVIA. There are certain places which have an effect on one. Certain places that touch one.

PHILIP. Yes, I know what you mean. I can't imagine experiencing a similar sort of self-revelation in Pimlico.

OLIVER. Knightsbridge maybe, but certainly not Pimlico.

PHILIP. In any case, my darling, I wish you'd informed me that we were having dinner tonight with a man who regularly hears voices. I'd have been more prepared.

SYLVIA. Oh, Philip, you're awful.

OLIVER. I feel positively embarrassed now.

SYLVIA. Oh, don't. He's just being silly.

They laugh and then there is a pause.

We ought to get a move on.

OLIVER. Yes.

PHILIP. We don't want to upset the Yugoslavians.

SYLVIA. God forbid. I have to fetch my cardigan. I'll only be a minute.

PHILIP. You can't possibly leave us alone. We'll have nothing to talk about.

SYLVIA. You could have fooled me.

PHILIP. Well, hurry along then.

SYLVIA. All right, all right, stop being a bully.

PHILIP. Hurry up.

*SYLVIA leaves the room and the two men are left alone.
There is a pause and then they both begin to talk at the same
time.*

I can't begin to tell you...

OLIVER. There's something that...

PHILIP. After you.

OLIVER. No, please...

PHILIP. I was just going to say I can't tell you what this job means to Sylvia. How much she enjoys working for you.

OLIVER. It means a great deal to me too.

PHILIP. I don't think she's ever thrown herself into a project with such zeal. And the timing was so fortunate.

OLIVER. The timing?

PHILIP. The commission. It's what she needed after everything that happened.

OLIVER. She did mention that she hadn't been very well.

PHILIP. Yes.

An awkward pause.

You know she used to be an actress, don't you?

OLIVER. She told me.

PHILIP. Before she took up illustrating.

OLIVER. Yes.

PHILIP. Only for a couple of years.

OLIVER. I wish I'd seen her on the stage.

PHILIP. Then she decided to give up. She said she was doing it for us.

OLIVER. Oh.

PHILIP. But I think it scared her in some way.

OLIVER. Scared her?

PHILIP. She was exceptionally good. It was rather terrifying how good she actually was. She would *become* these people. Enter these people's lives so fully, so completely. Her imagination, I suppose.

OLIVER. I can believe she was very good.

PHILIP. Of course, that whole world...

OLIVER. The theatre?

PHILIP. Not really her cup of tea, I don't think.

OLIVER. Wasn't it?

PHILIP. But she was very good. Instinct, I suppose, intuition. And empathy. Those sort of qualities.

OLIVER. Yes.

PHILIP. But I think it's wise.

OLIVER. Wise?

PHILIP. That she gave up, I mean.

OLIVER. Do you?

PHILIP. She's fragile.

There is a pause.

Have a lot of sleepless nights, do you?

OLIVER. I beg your pardon?

PHILIP. You said earlier. In your story. The oracle. You said something along the lines of one day there will be an understanding of certain things that will make all the sleepless nights we now have seem almost worthwhile.

OLIVER. Oh.

PHILIP. And I was just wondering if there's lots of them. Sleepless nights.

OLIVER. A few.

PHILIP. All those Bellyfinches floating around in your head no doubt.

OLIVER. Probably.

A long pause. Something has happened. Then SYLVIA *enters.*

SYLVIA. I'm ready.

PHILIP. It's about time.

OLIVER. You look lovely.

SYLVIA. Thank you, Oliver.

PHILIP *starts turning off the lights.*

I was thinking.

PHILIP. What?

SYLVIA. How important this evening is.

PHILIP. Is it?

SYLVIA. For me. For all three of us, really.

PHILIP. Why?

SYLVIA. Oh, I don't know.

PHILIP. Have you got the keys?

SYLVIA. Yes.

PHILIP. Come on then.

They make a move towards the door. As they move towards it, a MAN *enters the room. He is wearing a Nazi uniform. He is invisible to them but on his entrance he brushes up close to them.*

SYLVIA. What was that?

PHILIP. What was what, darling?

SYLVIA. I felt... I felt something.

PHILIP. You felt what?

The MAN *moves to the centre of the room and stands there silently.*

SYLVIA. Nothing.

PHILIP. Don't forget your coat.

OLIVER. It's not warm.

SYLVIA *picks up her coat. They open the door to leave.*

PHILIP. So why is tonight so important then?

SYLVIA. Don't mind me. Just thinking out loud.

OLIVER. Do that often, do you?

SYLVIA. That's all.

PHILIP. Mad as a hatter, Oliver.

OLIVER. Is she?

SYLVIA. Don't be a beast.

PHILIP. Mad as a hatter.

They close the door behind them. Slowly, a scene change happens imperceptibly, in semi-darkness. Perhaps some music could be played – something that could well have been played in the scene change of a 1950's production – something soft, elegant. A couple of changes to the room – maybe a giant modern photograph is revealed or a plasma screen appears – so that now this could be a modern flat decorated in a 1950's retro style. But the room is essentially the same, the changes are superficial and decorative. The 1950's music begins to meld into something new, something loud, maybe violent. All the while, the MAN *in the Nazi uniform remains in the centre of the room, still and silent.*

2008

Still in semi-darkness, OLIVER *enters, but he is now in his underwear. Behind him he drags a dressing gown. He sits on the floor somewhere in the room with the* MAN *standing over him, looking down at him. The lights return and the music comes to an abrupt end. For the first few lines, the* MAN *speaks in a German accent.*

MAN. Don't fucking look at me, you fucking piece of shit.

OLIVER. I'm sorry. I'm sorry.

MAN. You better be.

OLIVER. I'm sorry.

MAN. You never fucking look at me, you worthless piece of shit. What are you?

OLIVER. What am I?

MAN. What are you? Tell me what you are!

OLIVER. What am I.

MAN. You fucking tell me what you are, you fucking piece of human shit.

OLIVER. I'm a fucking piece of human fucking shit.

MAN. Yeah, das ist good. Now lick my fucking boots.

> OLIVER *bends over to lick the* MAN*'s boots, but before he gets there he stops.*

OLIVER. Okay, I'm sorry, I'm going to stop you.

MAN. Shut your fucking mouth.

OLIVER. No, seriously, can you just stop. Please. Time out. Stop. Abracadabra.

MAN. Abracadabra?

OLIVER. Yes. Please. Stop. Abracadabra. Definitely abracadabra.

MAN (*in his own rather camp London voice now*). You'll have to pay me.

OLIVER. Yes.

MAN. I mean, I spent two fucking hours trying to get here. From Earls Court.

OLIVER. Yes. The Victoria line. It broke down. You told me.

MAN. And I got wet. Soaking.

OLIVER. I'm sorry.

MAN. Soaking wet.

OLIVER. Yes.

MAN. You'll have to pay me.

OLIVER. Of course. Of course I'll pay you.

MAN. I came a long way.

OLIVER. I know.

> *Pause.*

I'm just not in the mood. I should never have called. I was bored.

MAN. Okay.

OLIVER. And a bit lonely.

MAN. A lot of them are.

OLIVER. I think I just drank a bit too much.

MAN. All right.

Pause.

OLIVER. Have a drink with me.

MAN. You're paying.

OLIVER. You might as well.

MAN. It's still pissing it down.

OLIVER. Have a Scotch.

MAN. Oh, go on then.

OLIVER *pours the* MAN *a Scotch and hands it to him. They sit in silence for a while and listen to the sound of the rain.*

OLIVER. You're very good at it. Convincing, I mean.

MAN. Oh.

OLIVER. The accent and everything.

MAN. Thank you.

OLIVER. You're welcome.

Pause.

The picture's good as well. On the website.

MAN. So they say.

OLIVER. Is the Alsatian yours?

MAN. My sister's.

OLIVER. Glad you didn't bring him along.

MAN. Yes.

OLIVER. Effective though.

Pause.

You an actor?

MAN. Was.

OLIVER. Thought so.

MAN. Couldn't really make ends meet.

OLIVER. Theatre?

MAN. Mostly. All over the place. Northampton. Bristol. Fucking Ipswich.

OLIVER. Rep.

MAN. Did an ad once though. Dog food. Made a mint.

OLIVER. I thought you looked familiar.

MAN. And the odd voice-over.

OLIVER. It's a hard life.

MAN. You're telling me.

Pause.

OLIVER. So what do you do now?

MAN. Oh, you know. Bits and pieces. This, for a start.

OLIVER. Of course.

MAN. Help out in a florist's twice a week.

OLIVER. Nice.

MAN. Teach drama.

OLIVER. Great.

MAN. That kind of thing.

OLIVER. Okay.

Pause.

My boyfriend's left me.

MAN. Oh right.

OLIVER. Third time this year.

MAN. Makes a habit of leaving you, does he?

OLIVER. But this time it's for real. Took his vinyls.

MAN. How long you been together?

OLIVER. Year and a half.

MAN. That's a lifetime.

OLIVER. It is, isn't it?

MAN. I've never managed anything longer than eight months.

OLIVER. Haven't you?

MAN. No.

Pause.

You sad about your boyfriend leaving you then?

OLIVER. Yes. Yes, I think I am.

MAN. Oh right.

Pause.

OLIVER. It's been three days.

MAN. Three days?

OLIVER. Since he left.

MAN. Oh.

OLIVER. I haven't really gone anywhere.

MAN. Right.

OLIVER. Just sat here. Thinking about stuff.

MAN. You'll get over it.

OLIVER. I don't know.

MAN. You get over things.

OLIVER. No food left. Have to make the trip to Tesco's.

MAN. You don't want to starve.

OLIVER. No.

MAN. You'll get over it.

OLIVER. Who knows?

Pause.

MAN. So what is it you do for a living?

OLIVER. I'm a journalist. I write.

MAN. Oh, nice.

OLIVER. Is it?

MAN. Proper job. Not like me.

OLIVER. If you say so.

MAN. Not like dressing up.

OLIVER. Freelance. Write for the *Mail* a lot.

MAN. Got to pay the bills.

OLIVER. Yes. About to start working on a new magazine though.

Pause. The sound of keys in the front door. It opens. PHILIP *enters. He sees* OLIVER *and the* MAN *and looks surprised.* OLIVER *jumps up.*

PHILIP. Fuck.

OLIVER. Shit.

PHILIP. Fuck it.

OLIVER. It isn't…

PHILIP. I thought…

OLIVER. Fuck.

Pause.

PHILIP. I thought you were going to Glasgow.

OLIVER. I cancelled.

PHILIP. You said you were going to Glasgow.

OLIVER. I didn't realise you still had keys.

PHILIP. You said you wouldn't be here.

OLIVER. I thought you left the keys.

PHILIP. I came to get the case. The last case.

OLIVER. Yes.

PHILIP. The books.

OLIVER. I know.

> OLIVER *notices* PHILIP *looking at the* MAN *and taking in the uniform.*

> This is...

PHILIP. It's fine. I'll be quick.

OLIVER. Take your time.

PHILIP. They're in the bedroom.

OLIVER. I know. By the bed.

PHILIP. I'll be quick.

OLIVER. Okay.

> PHILIP *hovers for a second, then darts out of the room and into the bedroom.*

> Fuck. Fuck, fuck, fuck, fuck, fuck, fuck. Please go.

MAN. Sorry?

OLIVER. Just go. Please. Go.

MAN. I've only just started my drink.

OLIVER. Just please go.

MAN. You haven't paid me.

OLIVER. Yes.

MAN. I'm not moving till you pay me.

> OLIVER *runs over to where his wallet is and takes out a few twenty-pound notes.*

OLIVER. There. Keep the change. Just go.

MAN (*counting the money*). I need to get out of this.

OLIVER. No. You really must go. It's important to me.

MAN. I'm not travelling on the fucking Victoria line dressed up as a Nazi.

OLIVER. You know where it is. Just be quick. Please.

The MAN *takes his bag and starts walking towards the bathroom, then turns around.*

MAN. He's not coming back to you.

OLIVER. Fucking get dressed.

The MAN *exits.* PHILIP *returns carrying a small suitcase.*

PHILIP. Got it.

OLIVER. Great.

PHILIP. I'll be off.

OLIVER. No.

Pause.

Please. Just wait. Just for a minute. A drink. That's all. Promise.

PHILIP. Not a good idea.

OLIVER. Please.

PHILIP. You have company.

OLIVER. Oh, him.

PHILIP. Yes.

OLIVER. He's just… he's…

PHILIP. You needn't explain.

OLIVER. Friend of Nick's. Fancy dress. Fancy-dress party. On his way to Nick's. Had a drink. That's all. He's leaving.

PHILIP. Nick's in Brazil.

OLIVER. Of course he is. I know that.

PHILIP. For fuck's sake.

OLIVER. I know Nick's in Brazil.

PHILIP. For fuck's sake, Oliver.

OLIVER. Yes.

Pause.

Please. Please just stay for a minute. Fifteen minutes. That's all.

Pause.

PHILIP. That man.

OLIVER. Yes.

PHILIP. That man is wearing a Nazi uniform.

OLIVER. I know. Weird, isn't it?

PHILIP. You must wonder sometimes to yourself: what's next?

OLIVER. Yes. I do. I do.

Pause.

Please stay.

PHILIP. I don't want to.

OLIVER. Please.

Pause.

The cupboards look empty.

PHILIP. What?

OLIVER. What I'm saying is I hadn't quite realised how many clothes you had.

PHILIP. Oh.

OLIVER. All of a sudden they look empty.

Pause.

You look well.

PHILIP. I haven't changed.

OLIVER. No.

PHILIP. It's been three days, Oliver. People don't change in three days.

OLIVER. Feels like longer. You look different.

PHILIP. Yes.

OLIVER. Like I've lost you.

Pause.

The thing is, Philip, I'm not sure I can live without you.

The MAN *returns from the bathroom dressed in his own clothes and carrying his bag.*

MAN. It's still pissing it down.

OLIVER. Right.

The MAN *walks over to the table and drinks down what's left of his Scotch.* OLIVER *and* PHILIP *just watch him.*

MAN. I don't actually mind the job. For the most part. You meet some interesting people. And there's definitely variety. I'd never be any good at the whole office thing. Hours and hours behind a desk staring at a computer screen. And I don't even mind travelling around London on the Tube and walking around in the pissing rain. But you do expect to be treated with a modicum of respect.

He walks towards the door.

I'm not asking for much, am I? I suppose it's what everybody's after. The thing is this, you see. I'm not a piece of furniture or a wind-up doll. I'm a human being. And I deserve to be treated as one. You can't just discard me like a piece of rubbish. I may dress up for your entertainment but I do have feelings, is what I'm saying.

(*To* PHILIP.) Nice to meet you.

He exits. A pause. Just the sound of the rain.

OLIVER. Some people.

PHILIP. I better go.

OLIVER *rushes to the bottle of Scotch. Pours him one.*

OLIVER. Just the one.

PHILIP *takes it reluctantly.*

Sit. Five minutes. Then you go.

They sit. Pause.

Had Sylvia on the phone this morning. Trying to console me. Bless.

PHILIP. How is she?

OLIVER. Sylvia? Oh, Sylvia's fine. 'I'll come by on Saturday,' she says. 'Come by with Mario. We'll go to Pride. Have a laugh.'

PHILIP. Pride?

OLIVER. On Saturday. I said… I said, 'I don't know if I'll be in the mood. Philip's gone. I don't… I don't know if he's coming back.'

PHILIP. I'm not, Oliver.

OLIVER. That's what I said to her. I said, 'Sylvia, I don't think he's coming back.' 'Well, you can't just sit there,' she said. 'Sit there being sad. We have to get you out. Out of the house. Cheer you up.'

PHILIP. What did you say?

OLIVER. I said, 'It's going to take a bit more than a park full of fairies to cheer me up.'

Pause.

I didn't love him, Philip. The American guy. I didn't love him.

PHILIP. I don't want to talk about it.

OLIVER. It's not love. I *love* you.

PHILIP. I'm going.

OLIVER. No.

Pause.

Okay. Here goes. There are things about myself that I don't understand. Things I want to but can't. It's as if it's something in me. Something in my DNA.

PHILIP. For fuck's sake.

OLIVER. With you it's different. With you it's love.

PHILIP. You lied to me.

OLIVER. It didn't mean anything. The other thing. You know that.

PHILIP. So why did you do it?

OLIVER. Because I need it.

PHILIP. You lied to me.

OLIVER. I know.

PHILIP. Over and over again.

OLIVER. Yes.

PHILIP. Fucking lying all the time. A year and a half of lies.

OLIVER. D'you remember when we met?

PHILIP. It's as if I don't know you.

OLIVER. At that party.

PHILIP. As if I don't know who the fuck you are.

OLIVER. At Sylvia's party.

PHILIP. Of course I fucking remember.

OLIVER. She knew we'd get on. She knew we'd fancy each other. There's this photographer, she said. Always travelling. You'll like him, she said.

PHILIP. I've got to go.

OLIVER. You'd just got back from Israel.

PHILIP. The West Bank.

OLIVER. Yes…

PHILIP. So?

OLIVER. So we talked. About your trip. About the photographs you'd taken.

PHILIP. Why the fuck are you saying this now?

OLIVER. I wonder what happened to that woman.

PHILIP. What woman?

OLIVER. The one you talked about. The one whose photograph you'd taken. The Palestinian woman.

PHILIP. Oliver.

OLIVER. You spent an hour describing her. You said her eyes were the blackest you'd ever seen and the most demanding.

PHILIP. Fucking hell.

OLIVER. Her son had died.

PHILIP. Why the fuck are you saying all this?

OLIVER. And I asked you what they were demanding.

PHILIP. So?

OLIVER. And you said they were demanding the dignity that comes with being heard. Not responded to. Just heard. The dignity that comes with being heard. The privilege of having a voice.

PHILIP. For fuck's sake.

OLIVER. That's when I recognised something in you.

Pause.

PHILIP. I'm leaving.

OLIVER. I felt a connection with you. There. At the party. And then here, when we came back. And now, I feel it now. I feel it now, Philip.

Pause.

And I think it's rare.

PHILIP. You're a cunt, Oliver. You're a stupid, stupid cunt.

OLIVER. Thank you.

PHILIP. You're welcome.

Pause.

A month and a half after we met, you fucking shagged someone.

OLIVER. I know.

PHILIP. I was in Brussels. The night before I went we were together. In that fucking bed. You saying I've never loved anyone like this. Then you drove me to Waterloo.

OLIVER. I know.

PHILIP. Eight – what? – ten hours after that, you're sucking someone else's dick.

OLIVER. I know.

PHILIP. What's that about, Oliver? What's that about?

OLIVER. I don't know.

PHILIP. To be fair, you told me. You said, 'I've done this thing. I don't know why but I've done this thing.'

OLIVER. I did tell you.

PHILIP. 'I've sucked a man's dick,' you said. 'In the park.'

OLIVER. I told you.

PHILIP. 'I could hardly see him,' you said. As if that made a difference. 'I could hardly see his face.'

OLIVER. It was dark.

PHILIP. 'I could hardly see his face.' You said that like it would make me feel better.

Pause.

The fact is, it depresses me. There. I've said it. The reason I can't stay with you. It depresses me.

OLIVER. Depresses you?

PHILIP. I did think about it. I thought maybe there's something wrong with me. Maybe I'm a fucking prude. A puritan. God knows. Maybe I should be a fucking priest. He never saw his face, I kept thinking. Sucked his dick, maybe…

OLIVER. Philip –

PHILIP. Sucked his dick, maybe, but never saw his face. Perhaps I'm the one who has the problem. They're not out on a date, they're not spooning, they're not planning their fucking holidays together, all they're doing is sucking each other off in a park. But it bothered me.

OLIVER. It's not your problem.

PHILIP. It's because we're men, I thought. That's what they say, isn't it? It's because we're men. It's not a gay thing. It's a man thing. Men need it.

OLIVER. That's what they say.

PHILIP. But all I know is what I felt. And that night, when I got back from Brussels, after you'd told me, I just lay in bed and looked at the ceiling. And I felt the loneliest I'd ever felt in my life.

OLIVER. I'm sorry.

Pause.

Sylvia's got that job.

PHILIP. What job?

OLIVER. That job she went up for. The Shakespeare. She said it's a break. The lead. Viola. *Twelfth Night*. Stratford.

PHILIP. She deserves it.

OLIVER. And Mario. The Italian boyfriend. It seems to be good. They're in love. He's a good man, she says. And very, very straight.

PHILIP. Good.

Pause.

OLIVER. I don't know what it is about me, Philip. Something about my name. It feels as if someone's calling me by my name.

PHILIP. What are you talking about?

OLIVER. The name I respond to. Like the other night. I'm walking by the gay place on the corner.

PHILIP. Right.

OLIVER. And I'm walking by it and I'm thinking, you need to go home, you need to work. Had to write a piece for the *Mail* on God knows what. The end of the world is nigh, that kind of thing. And I'm walking by the pub and it's as if this voice is calling my name.

PHILIP. Your name?

OLIVER. As if this voice knows my name. So I walk in. Coz this voice is calling me by my name. Have a couple of drinks. And there's a guy there… and he's not even good-looking. Actually, come to think of it, he's actively quite ugly. Big pot belly, that kind of thing. And you can smell the beer. You're six feet away from him and you can smell it. Wafting off his breath. And he's got a look in his eyes and he's looking at me as if he knows my name too. He's a bit pissed and he's leering… I mean *leering*, and I'm thinking, God, you're really kind of gross and next thing you know I'm actually standing next to him and he's telling me he's married and his wife's at her mother's for the week and he's kind of talking to me and rubbing his groin at the same time…

PHILIP. I'm not sure I want to hear the rest of this.

OLIVER. And the next thing I know we're in a cubicle. And I'm on my knees.

Pause.

PHILIP. Thanks for that.

OLIVER. It's an addiction is what I'm trying to say.

PHILIP. An addiction.

Pause.

OLIVER. There's something I never told you.

PHILIP. I'm beginning to miss your economy with the truth.

OLIVER. This thing that happened when I was young. Once, I must have been seventeen or something and I was staying at my aunt's. My mother's sister. The one you met.

PHILIP. Right.

OLIVER. And this woman came by. A friend of hers. And I was on my way out. So my aunt introduced me to this woman and I said hi, how are you and all that and then ran out. But a minute later I realised I'd left something. My sweater or something. So I ran back in the house to get it and then I realised that the two women – my aunt and her friend – were talking about me. But they hadn't heard me come back in the house. And I stood there, rooted to the spot. And listened. I couldn't hear everything but then – then this thing happened. I heard my aunt saying something along the lines of, 'He's a good boy but a bit of a lost soul.' Actually, it wasn't along the lines of. It was her exact words. I heard them. 'He's a good boy but a bit of a lost soul.' And the weird thing is – the weirdest – was that even before she said it, I kind of knew what she was going to say, like I'd heard her speak the words before, like her saying it and me knowing what she was going to say was all kind of tied up. Happening at the same time. 'He's a good boy but a bit of a lost soul.'

Pause.

PHILIP. I must leave.

OLIVER. Yes.

PHILIP. I can't stay.

OLIVER. No. You can't.

PHILIP. There is a part of you I'll always care about.

OLIVER. Thank you.

PHILIP. But this other thing… this thing you call your addiction. I can't deal with it.

OLIVER. No.

Pause.

PHILIP. Okay.

OLIVER. Yes. Yes. Okay.

Pause. PHILIP *stands. Picks up the suitcase.*

PHILIP. I'm sorry. I really am.

OLIVER. Don't go.

PHILIP. I have to.

PHILIP *walks towards the door. He stops and turns to*
OLIVER.

I still don't know why I hung around as much as I did. I was
thinking that on my way over. I mean, it's not as if I didn't
know. And yet I kept… I kept at it. I believed in something.
You. I don't know. I believed. I thought I knew you is what I
think I'm saying.

He leaves. OLIVER *is left alone in the room. He stands and
walks over to where the Scotch is to pour himself a drink.
Then, suddenly he stops. There is a gesture – a move of the
hand to the head, a bowing of the head, something – a
gesture that suggests aloneness.*

*He walks over to one of the light switches and turns off the
lights. In semi-darkness,* SYLVIA *emerges from the door
that leads to the bedroom. She is wearing a dressing gown.
The room reverts to its previous state.* OLIVER *slowly drifts
off, walking into the room that* SYLVIA *has just entered
from.*

1958

SYLVIA *comes to sit on the sofa. After a few seconds,* PHILIP *enters. He too is wearing pyjamas and a dressing gown.*

PHILIP. There you are.

SYLVIA. Darling.

PHILIP. I woke up. You weren't there.

SYLVIA. I had a dream.

PHILIP. One of your nasty dreams, darling?

SYLVIA. Yes.

PHILIP. All that Serbian food.

SYLVIA. Probably.

He joins her on the sofa. They sit in silence for a few seconds.

Did you enjoy yourself tonight?

PHILIP. I had a perfectly pleasant evening.

SYLVIA. Did you?

PHILIP. Drank a little too much of that awful wine perhaps.

SYLVIA. We all did.

PHILIP. But it was a nice enough evening.

Pause.

SYLVIA. You were quiet.

PHILIP. Was I?

SYLVIA. Not to start off with. Not at the beginning of the evening.

PHILIP. I thought –

SYLVIA. You were chatty before. In a good mood. But then during dinner you became quiet.

PHILIP. I'm sorry you thought I was quiet.

SYLVIA. I didn't mean it like that. It wasn't a criticism. Just an observation.

PHILIP. An observation?

SYLVIA. It didn't bother me... I just felt that you became slightly pensive. Melancholy.

PHILIP. That's a big word.

SYLVIA. Maybe as if something was bothering you.

PHILIP. I was listening, that's all. I felt I didn't have all that much to contribute, but I'm sorry you thought I was an awful bore.

SYLVIA. I didn't mean it like that.

PHILIP. No.

SYLVIA. I wish I hadn't said anything now.

Pause.

So you liked him then?

PHILIP. Liked whom?

SYLVIA. Oliver, of course.

PHILIP. He seems like a nice enough chap.

SYLVIA. Isn't he though?

PHILIP. I'm not sure that we have an awful lot in common, but he's a perfectly decent fellow.

SYLVIA. Why do you say that?

PHILIP. Why do I say he's a perfectly decent fellow?

SYLVIA. No, why do you say that you don't have a lot in common?

PHILIP. Because we don't. That seems clear enough.

SYLVIA. I thought you'd get on.

PHILIP. Well, it's true, isn't it? I mean, the man's a writer and all that. Very intelligent and outgoing, isn't he?

SYLVIA. Whereas you…

PHILIP. Well, I'm nothing like him, really. There isn't an artistic bone in my body.

SYLVIA. I don't know.

PHILIP. Anyway, what does it matter what I think of him? The point is the two of you get on famously and that's all that really matters.

SYLVIA. Well, I wanted you to like each other.

PHILIP. And the work, of course. That's important.

SYLVIA. Yes.

PHILIP. You seem to have discovered a way of understanding each other when it comes to the work and that's the most essential thing.

SYLVIA. I suppose so.

PHILIP. So what I think of him is irrelevant, really.

SYLVIA. Well, I wouldn't go that far.

PHILIP. The work is what matters.

Pause.

SYLVIA. You sound as if you loathed him.

PHILIP. I protest.

SYLVIA. As if you absolutely hated him.

PHILIP. I can't win with you, can I?

SYLVIA. Poor Oliver.

PHILIP. Why is it so important to you that I should like him?

SYLVIA. I think he'd be upset.

PHILIP. Why is it so important?

SYLVIA. If he even suspected how much you loathe him.

PHILIP. Now you're exaggerating.

SYLVIA. How you detest him.

PHILIP. Why is it so important?

Pause.

He has a manner to him, that's all.

SYLVIA. A 'manner'?

PHILIP. That's all.

SYLVIA. What sort of 'manner'? How do you mean, he has a 'manner'?

PHILIP. I can't put my finger on it.

SYLVIA. What sort of 'manner'?

PHILIP. I don't know. Just a manner.

SYLVIA. How do you mean?

PHILIP. We just don't have a lot in common.

Pause.

I don't know about you but I'm very, very tired.

Pause.

SYLVIA. I think of you, my darling, sometimes.

PHILIP. That's reassuring.

SYLVIA. No, I mean I think of you sometimes when you're at work. During the day, when I'm here. I'll be sitting in this very room, having my cup of tea or listening to the wireless, and I think of you at work. I see you in one of those large flats standing in the corner of the room in your brown suit as they look around. Then I see you locking those large doors behind you and walking down the road and back to the office.

PHILIP. What a strange thing to say.

SYLVIA. And I think you must be lonely. Philip must be lonely.

PHILIP. What a strange and funny thing to say, my darling.

SYLVIA. What you were saying tonight about not being happy in your work. About being envious of Oliver and me. I found it sad.

PHILIP. Oh, that.

SYLVIA. And I thought about you and the things that make you happy.

PHILIP. You needn't worry about me, darling.

SYLVIA. And I thought how terrible it will be if you never attain them. If you never hold close to you the things that really make you happy.

PHILIP. You needn't worry about me.

SYLVIA. Is there anything sadder?

PHILIP. You're exaggerating.

SYLVIA. Than a life lived like that?

PHILIP. You make me happy.

SYLVIA. And even if Dr Marsden is right –

PHILIP. Darling.

SYLVIA. Even if there isn't a reason –

PHILIP. We said we wouldn't –

SYLVIA. Even if we can, and will –

PHILIP. Sylvia.

SYLVIA. I'm wondering if that will –

PHILIP. We said we wouldn't.

SYLVIA. If it will make a difference.

Pause.

If having children will make a difference. To that.

Another pause. PHILIP *stands.*

PHILIP. Maybe you did have too much wine.

SYLVIA. We've never talked about it.

PHILIP. I think I'm going back to bed.

SYLVIA. Please don't.

PHILIP. I'm tired. And tomorrow's a long day.

SYLVIA. Please wait. Just for a moment.

PHILIP. I have to be up at seven.

SYLVIA. Stay.

Pause.

Please stay.

Pause.

SYLVIA. I should have felt relief when Dr Marsden said that he couldn't identify a reason we couldn't have children. He seemed to imply that if we just kept trying…

PHILIP. For God's sake, Sylvia…

SYLVIA. But then I started to question why I wanted it so much. A child. Why it meant everything to me. The desperation. Sometimes, I prayed with my whole body. I would lie next to you in bed and pray with my whole body to feel it… the beginnings of it. The stirrings. A new life inside me. I was sure I'd know the very night it happened.

PHILIP. For God's sake.

SYLVIA. And I thought it's natural, it's because I'm a woman. To be a mother. That's all. So I prayed and prayed and prayed.

PHILIP. What are you saying?

SYLVIA. But then I realised that there was something else. I wanted a child because I was frightened of us being left alone, Philip. The two of us. Just us. Alone.

Pause.

There was something I didn't tell you. Something that happened.

PHILIP. I don't understand you.

SYLVIA. Do you remember that actor I worked with?

PHILIP. Not now. Not the way you're speaking to me.

SYLVIA. Richard his name was. Richard Coveley.

PHILIP. Sometimes I simply don't understand you.

SYLVIA. He was in *The Cherry Orchard* with me. You came to see it.

PHILIP. What about him?

SYLVIA. He was tall and fair. He played Yepihodov.

PHILIP. I remember the play.

SYLVIA. You met him. After the performance one night we all went to have a drink together. We went to that little pub just off Shaftesbury Avenue. Do you remember?

PHILIP. Why are you telling me about this now?

SYLVIA. I liked him. He was a kind man. Unusual and quite private. But kind.

She pauses.

You didn't like him very much. I remember you said you didn't like him.

PHILIP. That was years ago. I met the man for a quick drink. There were many other actors there. I can hardly remember. Why is it important all of a sudden what I thought of this one man?

SYLVIA. You took exception to him. You said, I think you said, 'I find him offensive.'

PHILIP. I honestly can't remember.

SYLVIA. 'He offends me,' you said.

PHILIP. What has this to do with anything?

SYLVIA. You may have even called him mannered. Like you did Oliver tonight. You may have said he had a 'manner'.

PHILIP. I'm not quite sure of the significance of this conversation. But I'm very tired. Maybe you can explain to me in the morning what this is all about.

SYLVIA. Three days ago I read in *The Times* that he had killed himself. I didn't tell you at the time. I don't know why. But I didn't.

PHILIP. Well, I'm sorry to hear it.

SYLVIA. Maybe it's because I remembered that you hadn't liked him. That he'd offended you in some way.

PHILIP. You've obviously been very affected by it.

SYLVIA. He hung himself. There'd been a scandal. A court case. Gross indecency, that sort of thing.

PHILIP. I see.

SYLVIA. I think he was homosexual. I think Richard Coveley must have been a homosexual.

Pause.

When I read it I just thought of that night. Of why it was that you seemed to take such a dislike to him.

PHILIP. I can hardly remember the man. He seems to have made a lasting impression on you, but I can hardly remember the man. I'm very sorry that he's taken his own life and I'm sorry you seem to have been so upset by the whole affair but I hardly met the man.

SYLVIA. Why was it that you found him so repugnant?

PHILIP. I don't remember finding him repugnant. That's an exaggeration on your behalf. I found him mildly offensive, that's all. In a way that those men can often be offensive. Effeminate. I do recall him looking at me in a way I found overt.

SYLVIA. But even if he did look at you, even if he did, why would you find that so objectionable?

PHILIP. This discussion is absurd. You seem intent on upsetting me.

SYLVIA. I just couldn't fathom why it was that Richard
Coveley disgusted you so. And that's why I didn't tell you.

PHILIP. This is wonderful. You're accusing me in some
perverse way of being responsible for the death of a man I
met on one occasion for approximately twenty minutes.

SYLVIA. I'm not accusing you of anything, Philip. I'm just
asking you a question.

PHILIP. Well, I can't deny to you that I'm concerned. That you
seem to have regressed.

SYLVIA. I'm sorry you feel that way.

PHILIP. You're sounding alarmingly similar to what you
sounded like before Devon.

SYLVIA. Before my illness. That's what we decided to call it,
wasn't it? My illness.

PHILIP. Are you finished?

SYLVIA. As if it were a bad case of the flu.

PHILIP. Is there anything else you wish to discuss? Or am I free
to go now?

SYLVIA. I didn't mean to keep you here by force.

PHILIP. You asked me not to leave. You obviously felt a
burning need to communicate these disparate and disturbing
thoughts to me and I'm simply asking you if you've now
finished.

SYLVIA. Did Oliver offend you in the same way that Richard
Coveley did?

PHILIP. If you're asking me if I think Oliver Henshaw is a
homosexual, I really wouldn't know. I haven't given it a
moment's thought. His private life after all is none of my
business and neither do I think it should be any of yours. I
will try and explain to myself your somewhat strange
behaviour tonight by the fact that you have clearly been
upset by this man Coveley's death. This, combined with the
possibility that you had a few too many glasses of wine, can

go some way to justifying what can only be described as an outburst of irrationality. Now if you'll excuse me I really do need to return to bed.

SYLVIA. You didn't ask me about my dream.

PHILIP. Your dream?

SYLVIA. What woke me up in the first place.

PHILIP. I have a feeling you're going to tell me about it regardless of whether I want to listen or not.

SYLVIA. We were together. It was a field of sorts, out in the middle of nowhere. There was nothing there. No buildings, no people, no cars. I was frightened. Then we saw this tiny, tiny little light. We thought it might be a house, some sort of life was there. So we decided to run towards it. It was as if in the growing darkness this weak light signified everything that could help us survive. But the more we tried to run towards it, the further it moved away from us. And we kept running, though our feet were stuck in this mire, this quicksand, and my heart was beating so loudly, it sounded like a million pounding drums in my head. And then I turned and I looked at you but you weren't there. A man was there and he was wearing your clothes and was your height and the hair… the hair was like yours. But where there was a face, where there was supposed to be *your* face, there was nothing. It was blank. I couldn't find your face, Philip. No eyes, no mouth, nothing. I was alone. And then that light – the one we had been trying to move towards – even that disappeared.

PHILIP. Come to bed with me. You're tired.

SYLVIA. In a little while.

PHILIP. Goodnight.

SYLVIA. Goodnight, Philip.

PHILIP *exits and* SYLVIA *stays in the room alone. A few seconds pass and she slowly stands. She is about to follow him into the bedroom but then, suddenly, there is a gesture – an echo of* OLIVER*'s gesture from the end of the previous scene. An anguish. She leaves the room.*

OLIVER *enters and sprawls out on the sofa, still in his dressing gown. By his side is a near-empty bottle of Scotch and a glass. The lights are dim. The television is on and the room is full of the sound of* Big Brother *or something similar, contemporary. Then there is a knock at the door. He doesn't stir. The knocking becomes louder, more determined. Eventually he crawls to the door to open it.* SYLVIA *enters. She's carrying a bag of groceries.*

SYLVIA. Fuck.

OLIVER. Lovely to see you too.

SYLVIA. I thought you'd slashed your fucking wrists.

OLIVER. I have told you on numerous occasions that if I ever choose to follow the path to self-obliteration it will be noxious fumes.

She sweeps by him and disappears into the kitchen. She speaks the next few lines from offstage.

SYLVIA. You have fifteen minutes.

OLIVER. How very generous you are with your time. It's a good thing we're such good friends.

SYLVIA. Mario's just flown in. He's taking me out. And then I'm staying at his. Call me old-fashioned but I've missed him.

OLIVER. Sweet.

SYLVIA. I bought you food. Avocado mousse. Organic feta. Madagascan vanilla yogurt. Basics.

OLIVER. Thanks, Mum.

SYLVIA. I'm having a beer.

OLIVER. Help yourself.

She reappears at the kitchen door, beer in hand.

SYLVIA. What happened?

Pause.

OLIVER. He said I depress him.

SYLVIA. You depress him.

OLIVER. The anonymous sex thing. He said it depressed him.

SYLVIA. Okay.

OLIVER. So I told him it's not the same thing. I mean, when we're together... when I'm with Philip, that's different. But you know the other stuff, the park, the sauna, the internet, whatever, that stuff...

SYLVIA. The slut stuff.

OLIVER. The slut stuff, thank you, that's not the same. It's kind of... what's it like, it's kind of like going to the loo. Only with someone else.

SYLVIA. Like going to the loo with someone else.

OLIVER. Exactly.

SYLVIA *pauses. Her phone is vibrating.*

SYLVIA. Excuse me, I'm feeling a vibration in my nether regions.

OLIVER. Lucky you.

She takes out the phone and checks to see who it is.

Is that Pesto-breath?

SYLVIA. Racist.

She answers it.

(*On the phone.*) Hi. Welcome back. How was the trip?...

OLIVER. Say hi from me.

SYLVIA. Good... no, I'm fine. I missed you. I'm at Oliver's.

OLIVER. Say hi.

SYLVIA. Ollie says hi. Hello back. Yup. Okay. I won't be long.

OLIVER. He's eating into my time.

SYLVIA *makes a face at* OLIVER, *telling him to shut up*.

SYLVIA. I haven't got the car, I'll take the Tube. (*She looks at her watch.*) I can be there by nine. Or nine-thirty at the latest.

OLIVER. Tell him he's eating into my fifteen minutes.

SYLVIA (*to* OLIVER, *with her hand covering her mobile*). Please shut up.

OLIVER. I do beg your pardon.

SYLVIA (*on the phone again*). That sounds nice. Yummy. I'll see you then – call you from Hammersmith. *Ciao.* Welcome back. *Ti amo*.

She turns it off.

OLIVER. '*Ti amo*'?

SYLVIA. Shut up.

OLIVER. Vintage Cartland.

Pause.

SYLVIA. Okay, so let me try and get into Philip's mind here. Coz I think that's what we need to do. Devil's advocate kind of thing. Figure out what it is... what it might be that depresses him.

OLIVER. Be my guest.

SYLVIA. Okay, here goes.

OLIVER. I'm all ears.

SYLVIA. Okay, so you're walking through a park, it is nighttime and then suddenly you see this guy.

OLIVER. I'm with you.

SYLVIA. And he is gorgeous. I mean *gorgeous*. And he takes his dick out.

OLIVER. I like it.

SYLVIA. And it is big. I mean *big*. And he is waving it, nay, brandishing it in your face. And your urge –

OLIVER. My urge is to get down on my knees and give him satisfaction.

SYLVIA. Your urge, as you so succinctly put it, is to kneel down and give him satisfaction. But stop. Newsflash. You find out, after you've seen his man-tool but before you do the actual kneeling-down bit, you find out through some psychic newsflash something about him. A few facts. I don't know. Someone tells you this man is a racist. BNP or something. Or he sells crack to fourteen-year-olds. Do you still suck his dick? Do you still give him satisfaction?

A pause as OLIVER *thinks about it.*

OLIVER. When you say big, how big?

SYLVIA. Be serious. Do you suck his dick?

OLIVER. Probably.

A short pause.

SYLVIA. I'm siding with Philip on this one.

OLIVER. It's not like we're having a conversation. I'm not endorsing his world view. It's not like I'm saying it's okay, I love the BNP and of course I agree with you that the Holocaust never happened. I'm just sucking his dick, for God's sake, I'm not voting for him.

SYLVIA. Definitely with Philip on this one.

OLIVER. Anyway, the point is you pick the worst possible scenario. You say this man is a BNP freak and kills babies. Whatever. That's the exception. I mean, most of these men, most of the men in the saunas or whatever, are like you and me. I mean, why did you have to choose a BNP freak? Why couldn't it be a concert pianist who gives all his money to the Save the Children fund?

SYLVIA. It could be. But the point is – and I've got a feeling that this is the detail that depresses Philip – the point is *you don't know*. You don't know whose dick you're sucking.

OLIVER. Whatever.

Pause.

Are we playing the honesty game?

SYLVIA. I hope so.

OLIVER. The honest truth?

SYLVIA. And nothing but.

OLIVER. However unattractive?

SYLVIA. That's what friends are for.

OLIVER. In that case the honest truth is that not only I'd do it, I mean the cock-sucking thing, but I kind of really like it. The example, I mean. What you chose. The BNP example. Kind of turns me on.

SYLVIA. I knew you'd say that.

OLIVER. The fact is – oh, fuck, fuck, fuck, I wasn't going to tell you this, but when Philip came round, there was a man here and he was, fuck, I don't know how to say this...

SYLVIA. Just try.

OLIVER. Well, he was a Nazi.

SYLVIA. A Nazi? You had a Nazi over?

OLIVER. Not a real Nazi.

SYLVIA. How d'you mean, 'not a real Nazi'?

OLIVER. A make-believe one.

SYLVIA. A make-believe Nazi.

OLIVER. I mean, you know, from the internet. So they have these various costumes and you choose one and then they come over and... well, it's roleplay, really.

SYLVIA. Roleplay.

OLIVER. I mean, you can have *anything*. A Viking. An air pilot. A plumber.

SYLVIA. But you chose a Nazi.

OLIVER. And you roleplay. You know, kinky stuff. It's not serious. It's fantasy land.

SYLVIA. Okay, so. What's your part? I mean, he's a Nazi, but what are you? A Viking?

OLIVER. No, I'm just me.

SYLVIA. You?

OLIVER. Yeah, he's a Nazi but I'm just me.

SYLVIA. So you're in the middle of this roleplaying thing and Philip walks in on you.

OLIVER. Kind of.

SYLVIA. 'Kind of'?

OLIVER. Well, we'd stopped. I'd stopped it. We were just having a drink.

SYLVIA. You were having a drink with the Nazi?

OLIVER. Yes. And Philip came in.

SYLVIA. That's not good.

OLIVER. Thanks for that. I know.

Pause.

I was once looking through the personals in *Gay Times*. Long ago. Before Philip. And this one personal caught my eye. It went something like this: 'Gay man, thirty-three, non-smoker, into bondage, rape simulation, leather, rubber, chains, rimming, felching. Looking for romance.'

That's my life.

SYLVIA. And then you find someone.

OLIVER. Why do I have to choose?

SYLVIA. Maybe you don't. Maybe you just have to understand it. And then see.

SYLVIA*'s phone makes a vibrating noise again.*

Excuse me. More vibrations.

It's a text. She reads it; smiles.

OLIVER. Is that the Italian again?

SYLVIA. Might be. Shit, I've got to go.

He doesn't answer. She stands up and starts putting on her coat.

OLIVER. Sebastian called earlier. They've been given the green light for the magazine – the money's come through. Said it was going to do to gay literature what Marie Antoinette did for the guillotine. Widen its appeal.

SYLVIA. 'Literature'?

OLIVER. He uses the word in a broad sense. The printed word, he means.

SYLVIA. I was going to say.

OLIVER. Apparently they have the biggest names on board. BA, BMW, Gucci, Gap. You name it. The big boys. Everyone wants a piece of it.

SYLVIA. Well, you guys are cool. And have disposable income.

OLIVER. They want me in New York next week... They're already floating ideas by me: a Tom Ford interview. A gay rich list. Sebastian mentioned a possible piece on the men's cosmetic industry. That kind of thing. And they're flying me over club.

SYLVIA. Of course. Have they got a name?

OLIVER. A name?

SYLVIA. For the magazine.

OLIVER. *Blissful.*

SYLVIA. Okay.

OLIVER. And something else too. Apart from *Blissful*. Sebastian's recommended me for a one-off. Some lad-magazine editor wants to meet me tomorrow. A piece about gay sex for the straight reader. I'm intrigued.

SYLVIA. I'll call you in the morning.

OLIVER. Anyway, it's all good. Salvation. Wash the man right out of my hair. I need to keep busy. Otherwise…

SYLVIA. Otherwise what?

OLIVER. Otherwise I'm going under.

SYLVIA. 'Under'?

Pause.

OLIVER. I've never been this bad. Not ever. I mean it.

SYLVIA. Well, that should do the job. *Blissful.* And then there's your book, of course.

OLIVER. Book?

SYLVIA. Your fucking book, Oliver, remember?

OLIVER. Oh, that.

SYLVIA. I could have sworn you were writing a novel.

OLIVER. So like you to bring it up.

SYLVIA. Love. Life. Some sort of meaning. Or at least an effort to find it.

OLIVER. Fuck off.

SYLVIA. I am. Fucking off.

OLIVER. Cow.

She moves towards the door. She opens it.

SYLVIA. We'll talk.

OLIVER. I don't know.

SYLVIA. What? What don't you know?

OLIVER. What I want.

SYLVIA. What you want?

OLIVER. I don't know what I want any more. But it's not good.

SYLVIA. What isn't?

OLIVER. I'm scared.

A pause, and then:

I mean, I'm sitting here and I'm joking with you, but –

SYLVIA. But what?

OLIVER. I don't really see the point any more. And I have to figure it out. Otherwise...

SYLVIA. Otherwise what?

OLIVER. Who knows?

Pause.

I'm going to ask you the biggest favour. And it's not easy for me. But I have to do it. Just this once. Never again. You know I wouldn't. If I didn't have to.

Pause.

SYLVIA. Fuck.

OLIVER. Stay with me. Just tonight. Please, Sylvia.

SYLVIA. I can't.

OLIVER. Just this once. Please. Please. Please.

SYLVIA. No, Oliver.

OLIVER. I'd never ask. You know that. Not if I didn't feel I had to. Not if I didn't feel –

SYLVIA. Please don't do this.

OLIVER. Not if I wasn't scared of me.

SYLVIA. Scared of you?

OLIVER. Of being left alone tonight. Of being me alone tonight.

A pause as she lets these words sink in.

PHILIP *enters in his 1958 clothes; a ghost.* SYLVIA *can't see him and neither can* OLIVER, *but his presence, somehow, is felt. He emerges from the shadows.*

OLIVER. Somewhere inside me a feeling that… a kind of betrayal.

SYLVIA. Betrayal?

OLIVER. Yes.

SYLVIA. You're the betrayer or the betrayed?

OLIVER. Both. I don't know. Both.

SYLVIA. Okay. Take a deep breath. Start again. Try and make sense. I mean, articulate, for God's sake, and then maybe, *maybe*, I can start to help you.

OLIVER. I'm trying, you shit.

SYLVIA. Try harder.

OLIVER. I keep returning to this one same place. So I have to figure it out.

SYLVIA. What same place?

OLIVER. And I'm not threatening to wake up a born-again Christian or a Muslim or God knows what. Or shave off my hair and walk around Soho singing 'Hare Krishna'. But something needs to happen, some sort of realisation. Because otherwise, well, fuck me, it's untenable.

SYLVIA. What is?

PHILIP. Oliver.

OLIVER. The voice.

SYLVIA. What voice?

OLIVER. The voice that says –

PHILIP. Oliver –

OLIVER. You're no good –

PHILIP. Oliver –

OLIVER. You're unlovable –

PHILIP. Oliver –

OLIVER. This is what you deserve.

Pause. PHILIP *stands back into the shadows.*

SYLVIA. I'll call Mario.

OLIVER. I'm so sorry.

SYLVIA. So am I.

OLIVER. Thank you. Thank you. Thank you.

SYLVIA. I don't know why. I don't know *how* –

OLIVER. Thank you so much.

SYLVIA. – *how* you do it.

OLIVER. And then tomorrow you can spend the whole day with him. Morning, afternoon, evening.

SYLVIA. Thank you. For your permission, I mean. How generous.

OLIVER. Don't be mean.

Pause.

SYLVIA. I'm having another beer.

OLIVER. I'll get you one. Make yourself comfortable. *Mia casa, tua casa.*

He goes to the kitchen. SYLVIA *sits.*

SYLVIA. I can't keep doing this, you know. Ollie. Being here for you. Not like this. It's not fair. On either of us. I need to say that.

OLIVER. I'll never forget this.

Pause. The sound of him opening a drawer and then a bottle.

SYLVIA. The irony is that Mario can't wait to meet you. I talk about you all the time. He said he wants to come to Pride on Saturday. He's only ever been to the one in Rome. He swears he saw a priest throwing an egg but I think that's just his own brand of anti-Catholic propaganda. Did I tell you he wants to have a baby? I said, 'Not until I meet your mother.'

Her name's Filomena. Can you believe it? Filomena. Sounds like a bloody volcano. Apparently, her gnocchi is to die for.

Pause. She stands and walks over to the door that leads to the kitchen just as PHILIP *emerges again from the shadows and comes to sit in the chair she has just left.*

The thing is you need to sort it out yourself is what I'm saying.

PHILIP *stares ahead as if lost in his own thoughts. There is a knocking at the door. He ignores it for some time – it persists. Then, slowly, he stands up and walks towards the door just as* SYLVIA *disappears into the kitchen.* PHILIP *opens the door and* OLIVER *is standing there in his 1958 clothes. He is in a raincoat and soaking wet.*

1958

PHILIP. Hello.

OLIVER. I'm sorry.

PHILIP. You're drenched.

OLIVER. Yes.

   Pause.

   I wasn't planning to come. We said…

PHILIP. We said we wouldn't meet.

OLIVER. I know.

PHILIP. We said we'd try not to talk to each other.

OLIVER. Yes.

PHILIP. I think we both agreed it wasn't a good idea.

OLIVER. I know.

   Pause.

PHILIP. You're drenched.

OLIVER. I was absent-minded.

PHILIP. Soaking.

OLIVER. I left my umbrella in the library.

PHILIP. Well, you'd better come in.

OLIVER enters. He hovers.

OLIVER. I'm sorry.

PHILIP. Sylvia's in Wimbledon staying with a friend. She'll be back tomorrow.

OLIVER. I know. We spoke on the telephone. That's why I came.

PHILIP. I don't think it's a good idea.

OLIVER. I needed to talk to you, Philip.

PHILIP. I didn't realise there was anything else to say.

OLIVER. Just one last time. And then I won't bother you.

Pause.

PHILIP. Well, you'd better have a seat.

OLIVER. Thank you.

They sit facing each other. There is a long pause before
OLIVER *starts talking.*

I wanted...

PHILIP. What?

OLIVER. Nothing. I thought... I hoped...

PHILIP. You hoped what?

Pause.

OLIVER. I walked across the park. It was pouring with rain. I was forgetful. I'd been in the library. Trying to write. But I couldn't. I couldn't write. It's as if I don't know what I want to write. What I *have* to write. I left. To come here. But I was forgetful. I forgot my umbrella.

PHILIP. Yes.

OLIVER. I couldn't... I know we said... but I couldn't...

PHILIP. You couldn't do what?

OLIVER. All my life I've been waiting for some sort of confirmation that I'm not alone.

PHILIP. Yes.

OLIVER. When it comes, when that confirmation comes, you can't... I can't – I had to come here. And see you. I'm sorry.

PHILIP. For God's sake.

Pause.

OLIVER. It's funny. I thought I knew.

PHILIP. Knew what?

OLIVER. Knew what it meant to be lonely. To be alone. I thought I knew.

PHILIP. What do you mean?

OLIVER. But now. Now I know.

A long pause.

PHILIP. What is it you want to say to me?

OLIVER. That I love you.

PHILIP. Please don't say that again. I find it absurd.

OLIVER. I have no choice. It isn't a choice.

PHILIP. We agreed. You said... I asked you not to talk like that.

OLIVER. I love you so much.

PHILIP. Stop saying those words.

OLIVER. At night, I can't sleep. I see your face. I hear your voice.

PHILIP. Stop it.

OLIVER. When we were together, the last time, when we were together it did feel, didn't it, as if… as if. Did it not feel to you as if all of a sudden, everything, everything you *were* and are…

PHILIP. No.

OLIVER. I miss you.

PHILIP. I'd rather you left.

OLIVER. No. Please. One moment. Please let me stay for a moment.

Pause.

These four months… I understood something.

PHILIP. You understood what?

OLIVER. I used to think I was a sexual deviant. I used to –

PHILIP. Please, Oliver.

OLIVER. There was a place. Where certain men went. Where they went.

PHILIP. I don't want to hear this.

OLIVER. One of those places. I went. I stood outside. I watched. A part of me longed to go in. I can't lie to you, Philip. I longed and yearned to go in.

PHILIP. Please.

OLIVER. I used to think it was just a sexual lust. A physical need. A deviation.

PHILIP. It *is* a deviation.

OLIVER. That if I met the right girl, that if I married, if I had children, the physical need, the *sexual* need would stop. That if I loved a woman, if I could learn to love a woman, the physical need… I could learn to live without that.

PHILIP. It is a deviation.

OLIVER. That it would go away. That I could fight it.

PHILIP. That's right.

OLIVER. But then, when I met you…

PHILIP. You *can* fight it.

OLIVER. I knew it was more than that.

Pause.

That it was everything I am. Not something I can put away. Not just one part of me.

Pause.

When we were together. The times we met. All those times. When we talked.

PHILIP. We've been over this.

OLIVER. I realised that it was more. And that what I slowly learnt…

PHILIP. For God's sake…

OLIVER. Was that what happens between two people can be sacred. And important. And that it doesn't matter who those two people are.

Pause.

I remember being a boy. I remember having this dark, secret knowledge of what I pined for. Of who I was. It kept me up at nights. I was terrified. Everything, everyone, told me it was wrong.

PHILIP. It *is* wrong.

OLIVER. I thought so too. I believed that if the whole world told me so, the whole world must be right. Who was I to question that?

PHILIP. I don't see what it is you're trying to say.

OLIVER. I'm saying that when I met you, when I fell in love with you… I knew that it was true. That the world *was* wrong. That what I felt was honest and pure and good.

Pause.

I went in, Philip. Into one of those places I just told you about.

Pause.

I didn't care. I needed to go. I needed to *feel*... what it was like. My whole body, my whole being craved it. So I went. It was as if I was watching myself. There were men... there was this one man and he... I didn't know him. He didn't know me. We barely talked. Just a word. We didn't even really look at each other. And then... then it was as if I wasn't quite there. It was over in a couple of minutes. But it was as if I wasn't really myself. As if I was watching. Like a bystander. A witness. I can't describe it.

PHILIP. I think you should leave, Oliver.

OLIVER. But then when I... when we... it wasn't, it *isn't* the same. Because, you see, there was something *else*, Philip. We had spoken and I felt that I knew something of who you were. Your fears. Your loneliness. Your wants. I saw in your eyes, that you too, like me, are a good man.

PHILIP. A good man?

OLIVER. Yes, Philip, a good man. A *good* man. A good man. And it was the first time, when we were together, when we were embracing that I felt that I had a pride. A pride for the person I was.

PHILIP. Is this what you needed to tell me?

OLIVER. Yes, I suppose it is. I suppose I needed to tell you that what happened between us is not the same thing. Not the same as that place I went to.

PHILIP. It is the same. You're deceiving yourself. It's wrong.

OLIVER. And I thought that some of those men, if only you had seen them you would know what I mean, that some of those men, hovering, waiting in that dim flickering light, some of those men would also choose this, that maybe that's what many of them want, but because they don't know where... *how* to find it, and because they have been told that this is who they are, that they are these men who stand waiting to touch someone, to touch another man's skin, that they've believed that's *all* they are, but that what they want, what they really want is more than that, what they want is what we can have... an intimacy with someone they can hold onto for a while, that what they want more than anything is to be able to *see* them, to look at them, to look into their eyes and to *know* them. And be known.

PHILIP. Have you finished?

OLIVER. The way we know each other. Because from the minute I met you it felt as if you were the only person who had ever known my real name.

PHILIP. How do you mean?

OLIVER. As if we spoke the same language.

PHILIP. Like in your story.

OLIVER. Yes. Like in my story.

Pause.

PHILIP. But I don't feel the same way, Oliver.

OLIVER. Don't you?

PHILIP. No, Oliver, I don't. I don't. I don't.

Pause.

You see, Oliver, I love Sylvia. And Sylvia loves me. We're a couple and we love each other. What happened... I mean, what happened between us, between you and me, Oliver, between the two of us, that was simply a mistake. Call it what you will. A moment of weakness. A weakness. That's all.

OLIVER. But you said –

PHILIP. I may have said many things, Oliver, but unfortunately I probably didn't mean them. You see, I wasn't being myself. I was like a man possessed. I want you to understand though that I hold nothing against you. No rancour, no spite. I have some affection for you. I believe you are a decent man. I don't believe you influenced me or tempted me in any way or that your motives were malicious. I was as responsible as you were. We both made a mistake. That's all. I wish you well, Oliver. There are no hard feelings. But the memory of what happened... now that I seem to have regained my senses, the memory of what happened between us, of the things that happened between us, that memory fills me with shame. And disgust.

OLIVER. Disgust?

PHILIP. You came here today to persuade me that what we felt for each other, what you felt for me was noble and pure.

OLIVER. I did.

PHILIP. Well, you can feel that for me as a friend. And I can do likewise. I can like you and respect you, *try* to respect you, as a friend. But the other thing... that thing that you talk about... that place, those people.

OLIVER. What about them?

PHILIP. Those men... the ones you so eloquently described, Oliver. They are not like me and I am not like them. If you want me to be honest, Oliver, if you want to know the honest truth, I despise them. That isn't too strong a word. I have to be honest with you. I pity and despise them. I've seen them... I *see* them, I notice them in a crowd, on a bus, on the street and they disgust me. The way they walk, the way they look at you, all in the same way. I'm not like that, Oliver. And I don't think you are either. So we must put this behind us. It's for the best. I promise you it's for the best.

OLIVER. Is it?

PHILIP. One day you'll thank me. You'll understand that I did this to protect you in some way. From yourself. You'll understand that in my own, strange way it was my gift to you. My parting gift.

A long pause.

OLIVER. I suppose I should leave.

PHILIP. Yes.

Pause.

OLIVER. She knows, Philip.

PHILIP. Knows what?

OLIVER. She knows everything. About you. She knows
everything about you, Philip.

PHILIP. How do you mean?

OLIVER. About what keeps you up at night. About the stirrings
of your heart. The many things you're frightened of. The
lonely thoughts you have. You had said to me that what
made her such a wonderful actress were these two qualities
she had – her empathy and her imagination. They are the
same qualities that make her wise and generous. The
qualities that make her know you better than you know
yourself. And you have to now – because you will not be
offered another opportunity – you have to now ask yourself
why it is you repay her with the worst possible deception.
And I'm not talking about us. About what happened between
us. I'm talking about the opposite – I'm talking about your
refusal to acknowledge it for what it really is.

PHILIP. Please don't talk about Sylvia to me.

OLIVER. Why not?

PHILIP. I don't want her talked about in this way. Between us,
like this. I don't want us to discuss the subject of my wife.

OLIVER. Do you honestly think it's easy for me? I care about
her. Deeply.

PHILIP. I don't want to talk about it.

OLIVER. But then I understood that this is what she wanted.
Not *this*. Not how things are now. But us. The meeting. That
is what she wanted.

PHILIP. You're insane.

OLIVER. She brought us together, Philip. I know that she
brought us together.

PHILIP. You're mad.

OLIVER. Maybe not consciously, maybe not in full awareness of what she was doing. But I can put my hand on my heart and swear that Sylvia brought us together.

Pause.

I wonder when you first started thinking of emigrating.

PHILIP. Emigrating?

OLIVER. Yes. Emigrating. You mentioned it. The night I met you. Sylvia said the flat was strewn with books on Africa.

PHILIP. What has that to do with anything?

OLIVER. So I was wondering when it was that you started having that dream. Seventeen, eighteen, when? Maybe when you were becoming a man. Discovering yourself. Who you really were and what it was you wanted from your life. The open plains, you thought. The open plains of Africa. Not a bad place. I can see you there. This country is small. You need somewhere bigger. Somewhere to breathe. So you set off. I can see you. You said you never got further than Brighton, but I can see you miles, miles away. Across the cold waters of the Channel, down across the Mediterranean, down in Africa where you long to be. What are you doing there? Farming? Hunting game? Teaching? I suppose it doesn't really matter. In that sort of place, under that kind of sky you'll eventually discover what it is you're there for. In your own time.

PHILIP. Oliver.

OLIVER. I won't see you again then.

PHILIP. No.

OLIVER. That's what you want.

PHILIP. That's what we both need. To continue. To return to things as they were.

OLIVER. So what is the point?

PHILIP. The point?

OLIVER. What is the point of this stupid, painful life if not to
be honest? If not to stand up for what one is in the core of
one's being?

PHILIP. I don't know. I don't know.

OLIVER. Something's happened to me, Philip. I can't go back.
Not to how things were before.

PHILIP. What do you mean?

OLIVER. Don't worry, I'm not expecting you to come with me.
I'm not expecting anything any more. Not from you.

PHILIP. I'm sorry.

OLIVER. You're weak, Philip.

PHILIP. I wasn't...

OLIVER. What?

PHILIP. It isn't that...

OLIVER. Tell me.

PHILIP. No. Nothing.

OLIVER. Please tell me.

PHILIP. It isn't easy. It isn't easy.

Pause.

I wish I'd never met you. I wish she'd never brought you
here.

OLIVER. Who are you?

PHILIP. I don't know. Not any more.

OLIVER. You've never known. This was your chance to find
out. But you're not strong enough. You'll die, Philip, not
knowing who you are.

PHILIP. Be quiet

OLIVER. What a foolish, sad way to live a life.

Suddenly, PHILIP *strikes him across the face. It is a reflex; the reaction of a cornered animal.* PHILIP *is as shocked as* OLIVER, *who reels. There is some blood in the mouth.*

PHILIP. I'm sorry. Oh, God, I'm so sorry, Oliver. I'm so sorry.

He moves towards him; OLIVER *flinches.*

Let me see.

OLIVER *lets him.*

I'm so sorry, I'm so sorry, I'm so sorry.

OLIVER. It's all right. I'm fine.

PHILIP. I'm so sorry. I didn't... I'm so sorry...

OLIVER. I'm fine. Really, I'm fine.

And then, PHILIP *begins to cry. He collapses into* OLIVER*'s arms and begins to sob like a child.*

PHILIP. I'm sorry, I'm sorry, I'm sorry.

OLIVER. It's all right, Philip, it's all right.

OLIVER *comforts him. Then, a kiss. But* OLIVER *tries to remain tender.* PHILIP *has been taken over by something else – there is something urgent, aggressive stirring in him.*

OLIVER. Wait, Philip, wait.

PHILIP. No.

A struggle of sorts as PHILIP *pulls* OLIVER *over towards the sofa – his movement becoming more violent. He begins to pull at their clothes.*

OLIVER. No, Philip. Not like this. Not now. Not here. Wait.

PHILIP. Why not now? Why not here? It's what you want, isn't it? It's what you want me to be, isn't it?

PHILIP *has become violent. He throws* OLIVER *down.* OLIVER *is resisting.* PHILIP *unzips his own trousers and has managed to pull* OLIVER*'s halfway down. He mounts him with* OLIVER *resisting at first, then succumbing. In just a few, frenzied seconds he has ejaculated and the noise he* *makes at the moment of orgasm is a terrible, anguished cry of release. They lie on the floor for some time – PHILIP hiding his face in shame, OLIVER hiding his.*

Eventually, PHILIP stands. Quietly, methodically, he dresses and leaves the room. OLIVER does not move. He is lying on the floor, his face down against it. PHILIP returns a minute or so later. He pours himself a drink and sits. He lights a cigarette. A moment passes.

Slowly, painfully, OLIVER gets up and begins to rearrange his clothing. A minute or two pass in complete silence.

I knew you should never have come here.

Pause.

I think you should leave, Oliver. This thing… this thing is…

I want you to leave and never come back.

OLIVER *moves slowly across the room to the door. He does not look at* PHILIP. *He looks down at the floor. He opens the door, then pauses.*

OLIVER. I'm sorry… I…

He pauses, confused. As if trying to gather his thoughts.

What I… the thing… I… was…

Pause.

I'm sorry. I thought I knew you.

He leaves the room, closing the door behind him.

PHILIP *does not move. He remains seated, drinking his whisky and smoking his cigarette.*

The lights gradually fade.

End of Act One.

ACT TWO

2008

An office. Behind the desk sits PETER. *A bit of a wide boy.*
OLIVER *is sitting on the other side of the desk.*

PETER. So I'm talking to Seb Nichols and he says, 'If you're
looking for a good queer writer, I know the best one in
town.' Is that all right? I mean, using that word, the word
'queer', is that all right? No offence, I hope.

OLIVER. No offence taken.

PETER. Coz you never fucking know, do you? I mean, if you're
using the right word. I mean, I know the whole political
correctness thing's over – what the hell was that about? – but
I'm not the kind of guy who enjoys offending people. Thing
is, you never know what the right word is. I thought the word
queer might be to you guys what the N-word is to blacks. All
right amongst yourselves, but...

OLIVER. Queer's fine, queer's fine.

PETER. Pushing out the boundaries, that's what I'm talking
about. I don't know if you happened to see the piece we did
on Iraq.

OLIVER. No, I missed that.

PETER. This young kid gets back from the war and he's lost
both his fucking arms. And we follow him for a week, I
mean, it's like his diary or something, you know, stuff like
how his life has changed and all the shit he has to deal with,
stuff like his girlfriend walking out on him, and little shit too,
everyday things like using a cashpoint and how the fuck he
gets from A to B and this piece is very moving, I mean, it
pushes people's buttons, makes them think. Powerful.

OLIVER. I'm sure.

PETER. Coz there's more to life than tits and arse, tits and arse, tits and arse with a little football thrown in for good measure. And I'm not saying we're gonna turn into the *New Statesman* overnight, but we've got a wide readership out there, and most of them are impressionable young lads and, you know what they say, with power comes responsibility and all that.

OLIVER. So they say.

PETER. Coz the thing is, Oliver, most of these lads just love sex. Fuck, most of them would fuck a pig. And you know what I'm saying about 'times are changing', I mean, they are, believe me. The other night I'm out with all these mates and this one guy, his name's Dave and he's a bit of an arsehole but not a bad guy, and he's had a few and he's telling us about his trip to Thailand and he's left his girlfriend back at the Shangri-La or wherever the fuck they're staying at and he's walking the streets and feeling horny, as you do, and next thing you know he's having his dick sucked by a lady-boy. A fucking lady-boy. So he's telling us this and we're all fucking, 'You did what?' and he's saying, 'Best fucking blowjob I ever had,' and we're all taking the piss and everything and having a laugh, and two minutes after that we're all playing snooker again and the thing's forgotten. That wouldn't have happened ten years ago, times are changing, Dave would have kept that to himself. I mean, who gives a fuck these days? I mean, at the end of the day, Oliver, and forgive me if I sound crude, but if you've got a problem with it don't look down.

OLIVER. Fair enough.

PETER. So I'm thinking, come on, let's push the boat out here, nothing to be afraid of, lads, we're all fucking human after all, and you don't have to fucking get married or anything. Time to say to these lads it's okay if you get turned on by it, and it's cool to be gay or whatever and fucking face your homophobia or get over it. So what I really want is a piece on gay sex, I don't mean all the details but kind of the whole thing of sex in public and that kind of thing, making them a bit jealous, you know, kind of saying, well, if you could just walk into a park or a fucking public loo any time of the day and there's these gorgeous girls just waiting to be shagged, wouldn't you be up for it? Kind of like gay sex for the straight man.

OLIVER. Gay sex for the straight man.

PETER. So really what I want to do is a piece which will make them identify in some way and at the same time say, 'It's okay to be gay.' Change the way you think. Gay is cool. That kind of thing. These gay guys know what they want and they know how to get it. Innovators in various fields – music, fashion, fucking dogging. And just by putting that into the magazine – just by having it there – you are making people change their minds. Coz it's not every lad's magazine that does a piece on gay sex. It's what I was saying at the beginning – breaking down barriers.

OLIVER. Yes.

PETER. And basically what I'm saying is, if I can do my job and do the right thing at the same time then that's a good thing. And breaking down barriers is a fucking important part of that. Coz you guys fucking deserve it.

Pause.

I mean, you guys fucking fought for your rights. You had a lot of shit to fight against. A lot of fucking ignorance.

OLIVER. Sure.

PETER. I'm not gonna deny to you, Oliver, that I've got a personal connection. I mean, to the whole gay thing. The gay cause, if you like. Had an uncle.

OLIVER. Don't they all.

PETER. No, but I fucking did. Great bloke. Fucking ace. My mother's brother. Uncle Harry. Fucking lovely man. Heart of gold. Couldn't hurt a fly. Worked for the council. Fucking AIDS got him.

OLIVER. I'm sorry.

PETER. Seared on my memory. Fucking engraved. This one day. Last time I saw him. And he's dying. And I'm, what? Twelve, thirteen. And my mum takes me and my little bro to the Royal Free coz that's where he is. Some special ward and they don't really know what it is, I mean, they know it's AIDS but this was the early days, I mean, you didn't really know if you could catch it, *how* you could catch it, so my mum's like throwing the glasses away, you know the ones he's drunk out of after he's been to ours, not in front of him, of course, but after he's gone, and it sounds fucking ignorant but you didn't really know what was going on back then. So we get to the Royal Free, this special ward, like, and Uncle Harry's under this fucking sheet thing, like a special sheet with wires coming out of him and drips and stuff. Fucking mad. And he's on a ventilator coz he can't fucking breathe and it's making this noise, I mean, enough to drive you mad, this kind of wheezing noise, like the sound of death. Never seen anything like it. And it's all a bit weird and I lean forward and I'm a bit freaked out by the whole thing and my mum's saying, 'Say hello to your Uncle Harry,' but what she really means is, 'Say goodbye to your Uncle Harry,' coz we all kind of know he's on his way out so I lean in and this fucking sheet thing is between us, but I look down and I see and. Fuck. Fucking hell. His eyes. Like every other part of him is dying but his eyes. Windows of the fucking soul. That kind of thing. Eyes full of fucking love. Breaks my fucking heart.

Pause.

So we're turning around to go and there's this guy sitting there, a few feet away from us and he sees me and smiles and I'm a bit like, 'Who the fuck are you?' coz I'm twelve or whatever and don't know any better and my mum kind of drags us out of the place and I'm asking her who that guy was and she's like, 'That's your Uncle Harry's friend.' And later I found out that they've lived together for twenty-five years. Fucking twenty-five years. I mean, that's a long fucking time. I mean, that's fucking serious. So I'm asking my mum why we've never met him, how come we've never met Uncle Harry's friend before and she doesn't really have an answer. 'We just haven't,' she says. People are weird.

Pause.

So that's my own personal connection. I mean, to the gay thing. Uncle Harry. I want to honour that.

OLIVER. Thank you. I mean, thank you for sharing that.

PETER. So what I'm thinking, Oliver, it's been great to have this initial chat and I'll e-mail you some more ideas. About the kind of thing I'm after. But the main thing is to keep it light. And kind of exciting.

OLIVER. Exciting.

PETER. And you're all right about the money.

OLIVER. Four grand.

PETER. Two up-front.

OLIVER. Yes.

PETER. And two on completion.

OLIVER. Great.

Blackout.

1958

The park. There is a bench. When the lights go up we find OLIVER *and* SYLVIA. *They are standing. It is an autumn afternoon.*

SYLVIA. Thank you for coming.

OLIVER. It's a pleasure. It's been a long time.

SYLVIA. I thought you might find it odd that I asked you to meet me here. In the park. But the weather is being so kind and it all looks…

OLIVER. It looks beautiful.

SYLVIA. And I needed to get out, really. I've been spending ever so much time at home these days. Sometimes you forget that there's a whole world out there. Other people.

OLIVER. It's a lovely place to meet.

SYLVIA. And what with Philip being away so much. He's very busy. All of a sudden, work seems to take up all of his time. So it's nice to get out.

OLIVER. You look well.

SYLVIA. Do I?

Pause.

I walked by Hatchards the other day. Our book was in the window display. I felt so proud for a minute. So very, very proud.

OLIVER. You should.

SYLVIA. I do hope we get to work together again, Oliver. I hope that's not forward of me.

OLIVER. Not at all.

SYLVIA. Asking you, I mean. But I've plucked up the courage because it was important to me.

OLIVER. Of course we'll work together again.

SYLVIA. I thought maybe you were disappointed.

OLIVER. Disappointed?

SYLVIA. Oh, you know. That when it was actually over, that when the book was done and dusted maybe it didn't quite live up to your expectations. That it was a disappointment. My work, I mean, my contribution.

OLIVER. Not at all.

SYLVIA. That maybe it didn't quite live up to its initial promise.

OLIVER. You musn't think that, not for a minute. I couldn't have been happier.

SYLVIA. I suppose I was trying to come up with a reason why we hadn't seen each other for such a long time.

OLIVER. I've just been very busy.

SYLVIA. Of course.

OLIVER. But I'm so sorry if I gave you the wrong impression. Nothing could be further from the truth.

SYLVIA. Thank you for putting my mind at rest. That little part of me that remains sensible kept trying to tell me that it wasn't the case.

Pause.

I'm sure Philip thinks I'm completely mad most of the time.

Pause.

Your friendship is very important to me.

OLIVER. Are you all right, Sylvia?

SYLVIA. When I worked in the theatre there were a few people with whom I felt a similar kind of bond. There were people I could talk to openly about things which seemed vital and interesting and maybe even personal. Things I couldn't really talk to most people about. Even Philip. Especially Philip.

OLIVER. That's the theatre for you.

SYLVIA. And then when I met you I felt the same thing. That we didn't belong within that absurd little world in which talking about anything remotely significant seems an affront to one's dignity. A kindred spirit. Somebody you know you can be frank with and whom you hope can be frank with you.

She sits. A pause.

I'm lonely.

Pause.

Is that a terrible thing to say?

OLIVER. Not at all.

SYLVIA. I mean, I'm a married woman. I live with my husband. But sometimes I wake in the middle of the night and I lie in bed thinking how lonely I am. And the loneliness I feel is like a blanket. But not a blanket that comforts you. Something darker. More oppressive. It feels almost as if it stops me from breathing. I'm so sorry.

OLIVER. What are you sorry about?

SYLVIA. Calling you here. You were at home, writing probably, minding your own business and then you are summoned to the park to hear the ramblings of a mad woman.

Pause.

He frightens me, Oliver. I think that anything that is not let out will turn in on you in the end and destroy you. And those around you. An inverted, frustrated power. Do I sound insane?

OLIVER. No. No, you don't.

SYLVIA. There are things you suspect. And then, you brush them aside. Things maybe a part of you knows but to acknowledge them renders your life a lie. And then...

OLIVER. Then what?

SYLVIA. Then the foundations of everything you've ever depended on, the ground you've moved on, the home you've built for yourself, everything, the walls, the furniture, the air you breathe, everything seems unreal. And you cease to be able to distinguish truth from lies. Or at least from something you know is *not* the truth. An appearance of sorts. Life becomes a little like some horrible fancy-dress party. And it becomes unbearable.

Pause. Slowly, SYLVIA *starts to look through her bag for something.*

I found something of yours.

OLIVER. Of mine?

SYLVIA. At home. It must have fallen out of your pocket. I was wondering when it was. Three times you've been to our flat. Once, that first time when we asked you over so that you could meet Philip. The night we went to the Italian restaurant. And then twice after that. That morning you came to look at that last batch of illustrations when I couldn't come to yours because I had that awful cold. And then

ight of the party for the book's launch and that
've minutes when you dropped me off and we
⌐ brandy. So only three times when I was there.
then, of course, on all those occasions you were only in
the living room, unless of course you visited the bathroom,
which to be honest I can't remember.

She pulls out a pen from her handbag.

Your gold pen. The one you love so much. The one your
sister gave you. It was behind the cushion on the armchair.
The green armchair in our bedroom. It must have fallen out
of your jacket. You always kept it in the inside pocket, didn't
you?

OLIVER. Yes. Yes, I did.

SYLVIA. So it must have slipped out.

OLIVER. Yes.

SYLVIA. I assume it was the time I'd gone to visit my mother. I
was away for at least a week, wasn't I?

Pause.

Take it, Oliver. It's yours. It's your pen.

He takes it. There is a long pause.

I want you to know I don't blame you. I really don't. I did
think it hurtful and disturbing that you should choose… I
found it disturbing that you would… knowing that you have
a flat, that you have your own flat, that you would choose…
Isn't it funny that it should be that which upset me more than
anything else? I suppose because it was the only aspect of
the whole affair that surprised me. Your choice of location.
How absurd.

Pause.

But then, you see, I thought about it and even that I don't
blame you for. Because when one lives within that world of
lying, of deception, then the details begin to blur. One's
discernment is undermined I suppose is what I'm saying.
One's sense of judgement. So under normal circumstances

perhaps you wouldn't have chosen to insult me in that particular way. I like to think that.

Pause.

There are things I don't understand. It's a whole new territory for me. I'm trying so hard. It's not easy, but I'm trying. I love Philip so much, you see. I want him to be happy. And I want to be happy myself. Is that such a terrible thing? To want happiness.

She suddenly begins to cry.

OLIVER. I'm so sorry.

SYLVIA. All that wasted time. And I look at myself now, in the mirror and my face is the face of a woman who's forgotten herself and has been forgotten.

Pause.

Are you still in touch with Philip?

OLIVER. No. No, we're not.

SYLVIA. Was that his choice or yours?

OLIVER. His. I would have chosen the same as you.

SYLVIA. The same as me?

OLIVER. To live an honest life.

SYLVIA. An honest life.

OLIVER. Yes.

Pause.

SYLVIA. Was he happy?

OLIVER. Happy?

SYLVIA. Tell me. Was he happy? For an afternoon, at least. A morning. Was he ever happy?

OLIVER. I can't… I find it…

SYLVIA. Difficult. You find it difficult.

OLIVER. Yes, I...

Pause.

Maybe once. For a very short while. When for a very short
time he glimpsed the possibility of being... of being...

He pauses.

SYLVIA. Of being brave.

OLIVER. Yes. I suppose that's the right word.

SYLVIA. That thought filled me with a rage. Your happiness.
For a day or two I hated you so much. Because I suspected
then that even in your few, illicit meetings, in that very short
time you describe, he would have been able to be his real
self, something he has never been with me. In that glimpse
you talk of.

Pause.

OLIVER. I'm so sorry. I'm ashamed.

SYLVIA. I know you are.

Pause.

OLIVER. What will you do?

SYLVIA. I don't know. I honestly don't know. I wish I did.

OLIVER. I want to help you.

SYLVIA. I know. You are.

Pause.

I hope...

OLIVER. Yes...

SYLVIA. I hope with all my heart you find what you're looking
for. It isn't easy, I'm sure. You must be lonely too.

OLIVER. Yes, I am.

She moves to go, then stops.

SYLVIA. That first night when you came over, something
happened, didn't it? I felt it. I wonder what that is. It was

thick in the air. I want to feel that too. And someone to feel that for me. Goodbye, Oliver.

SYLVIA *walks away, leaving* OLIVER *sitting on the bench. The lights fade to black.*

2008

SYLVIA*'s flat. She's just opened the door.* OLIVER *is there. There's some blood in his mouth.*

SYLVIA. Fuck.

OLIVER. You really need to stop greeting me like that. I'm starting to take it personally.

SYLVIA. Jesus.

OLIVER. That's more like it.

SYLVIA. You're bleeding.

OLIVER. As ever, your powers of observation astound me.

SYLVIA. What are you doing here?

OLIVER. I was in the area.

SYLVIA. What happened?

OLIVER. An accident.

SYLVIA. An accident?

OLIVER. Could we discuss the details after I've stopped dripping blood onto your floor?

SYLVIA. What have you done?

OLIVER. It's a cut, that's all. A piece of kitchen roll will suffice, Miss Nightingale.

SYLVIA. Sit.

He sits. SYLVIA *runs into the kitchen to get the paper.*

OLIVER. It was my farewell tour. Let's call it a souvenir. One of my many fans. But this one had a predilection for the darker side. It seems you have the gift of prophecy, Miss Burton. Don't quite know what his voting profile was but I wouldn't have him down as a woolly liberal. A primitive man, I think it's fair to say. In a pinstriped suit though and he had shaved, I'll give him that. Shiniest brogues you've ever seen. You never can tell these days. I mean, he didn't look like he'd crawled out of a cave. Though the sweat was just about detectable under a velvety surface of Acqua di Giò.

SYLVIA *runs back with some kitchen roll. She gives him some to wipe his nose with.*

SYLVIA. I thought you said that whole aspect of your life was becoming untenable.

OLIVER. I was just checking.

SYLVIA. That was a conversation we had yesterday.

OLIVER. As recently as that?

SYLVIA. I thought you'd give it at least a week.

OLIVER. Obviously your powers of persuasion are not quite as effective as the lure of city cock.

SYLVIA. What the fuck happened?

OLIVER. I love a man in a suit.

SYLVIA. Clearly.

OLIVER. The signs were all there. During the actual act the whole verbal thing was slightly more convincing than usual.

SYLVIA. What verbal thing?

OLIVER. His use of adjective was alarming. And his imaginative use of the common noun left me speechless. It wasn't, of course, the only thing that made it difficult for me to put a word in edgeways.

SYLVIA. Spare me the details.

OLIVER. And then upon completion there was a push. Along the lines of – out of the way, I have important things to get on with: my friends are waiting, I'm taking my wife out to dinner, the markets are closing. That sort of thing. It was definitely just a push.

SYLVIA. You're bleeding.

OLIVER. It was the Rolex. One of the chunky ones. Caught my upper lip at an unfortunate angle. But it was a push. Not a punch.

SYLVIA. Well, that's all right then.

OLIVER. Hence my use of the word 'accident'. He was back in the office before I'd even realised what had happened.

SYLVIA. I'm sure if he'd noticed he would have driven you home in his Jaguar.

OLIVER. Without doubt.

Pause.

SYLVIA. Fuck, Oliver.

OLIVER. I was doing research.

SYLVIA. 'Research'?

OLIVER. The piece on anonymous sex. God knows why they chose me.

Pause.

Speaking of being surrounded by a sea of my gay brethren, I need to talk to you about tomorrow.

SYLVIA. Pride?

OLIVER. Yes. I'm not coming. Send my apologies to the Italian.

SYLVIA. You *are* coming.

OLIVER. Really, I'm not. I intend to spend the day in bed, nursing my wound.

SYLVIA. I spoke to Philip.

OLIVER. Liar.

SYLVIA. He said he might drop by. For me, he said. I told him you'd be there. He said that's okay, we're adults, we can cope. Something like that.

OLIVER. Are you being serious?

SYLVIA. Why would I lie?

OLIVER. Coz you're ruthless in the pursuit of your objectives.

SYLVIA. He's coming. Join us if you like. Or you could stay in bed having thoughts of loneliness and death.

OLIVER. Thanks for that.

SYLVIA. Let me know. I have to know how much food to make.

OLIVER. But the whole thing is so passé. All those tight T-shirts, all those preening queens. Anyway, what's the point? Remind me. Is it a demonstration, a celebration or a fashion show?

SYLVIA. Cynic.

OLIVER. Ten thousand mincers admiring each other's biceps. How could I be so dismissive.

Pause.

You look nice, by the way.

SYLVIA. Thank you.

OLIVER. Expecting visitors?

SYLVIA. A visitor. Singular. Yes, I am.

OLIVER. Okay.

SYLVIA. He's coming for dinner.

OLIVER. You cooking?

SYLVIA. Yes.

OLIVER. Smells good.

SYLVIA. Thank you.

OLIVER. Nothing Italian, I hope. He'll compare it to his mother's. That's what they do.

SYLVIA. Do they?

OLIVER. Hope you've stuck to something English. Frozen peas, that kind of thing.

SYLVIA. He'll be here any minute now.

OLIVER. That's exciting.

Pause.

So what else did he say?

SYLVIA. Philip?

OLIVER. No, Tom Jones. Yes, Philip.

SYLVIA. We talked about books.

OLIVER. Books?

SYLVIA. He told me about this book he'd been reading. Something Hungarian.

OLIVER. But he didn't say anything about me.

SYLVIA. No. Apart from what I just said. It'll be okay to see you, he said.

Pause.

OLIVER. Fuck you. You know how to push my buttons.

SYLVIA. Of course I do.

OLIVER. You know I'm coming.

SYLVIA. Of course I do.

OLIVER. I want to see him again. Be with him.

SYLVIA. He's a special person. Profound, honest, loyal.

OLIVER. Deeply compassionate.

SYLVIA. And handsome to boot.

Pause.

OLIVER. Sometimes…

SYLVIA. What?

OLIVER. Do you ever get that thing?

SYLVIA. What thing?

OLIVER. When you've just fallen asleep, just before the dreams begin. Or maybe just after you've woken up and your eyes are open even though your mind might still be dreaming.

SYLVIA. What about it?

OLIVER. The brevity of life strikes you. The brevity. The randomness. A flash in the pan.

SYLVIA. I've had that.

OLIVER. And I kind of feel then that the only thing that matters is finding some meaning, some reason, something you can slap the face of brevity with. And say I was here. I existed. I was. And then I think that the only two ways to do that are through work and relationships. How you changed people. How people changed you. And how you held on. To each other. Or at least gave it a damn good try. That's what defines your flash in the pan.

SYLVIA. Amen.

Pause.

So what do you do?

OLIVER. What do I do?

SYLVIA. There's only one thing you can do.

OLIVER. Which is?

SYLVIA. You have to stop sucking his dick.

OLIVER. Whose dick?

SYLVIA. You have to stop sucking the dick of your oppressor.

OLIVER. That's deep.

SYLVIA. Of your Nazi-Rolex man.

OLIVER. Sounds like a City Lit course. 'Marxist Theory for the Promiscuous Homosexual.'

SYLVIA. But one day soon you'll look up at the fascist whose dick you're sucking and you'll say something like –

OLIVER. 'Now look here' –

SYLVIA. 'Now look here, Klaus or whatever the hell your name is, surprisingly enough your dick is marvellously big but I have decided, a little like those pioneering fish that crawled out of the deep, dark ocean so many zillions of years ago, that from now on I will only suck the dicks –

OLIVER. Of social workers and yoga teachers.

SYLVIA. – of people who I know for a fact or at least *suspect*, for God's sake, aspire to things like justice, equality, mutual respect. And I really need to make this evolutionary leap, otherwise God knows where I'll end up.'

OLIVER. In the gutter. Or a cage. In an existential gimp mask.

Pause.

SYLVIA. I'm glad we've sorted that out. And now I have to…

OLIVER. You have to what?

SYLVIA. Mario will be here any minute and I need to, you know, get ready. That sort of thing.

OLIVER. Are you asking me to leave?

SYLVIA. Well, I mean, you can stay for a quick drink and meet him, but –

OLIVER. But what?

Pause.

SYLVIA. The thing is this. It's not that I don't enjoy being there for you. Sometimes. Because I do.

OLIVER. Sometimes?

SYLVIA. I need a little space, Oliver. And I don't mean just tonight.

OLIVER. Space? How d'you mean, you need a little space?

The question hangs.

I'll fuck off then, shall I?

SYLVIA. You know how when you stay, when you're around you take over in some way.

OLIVER. 'Take over'?

SYLVIA. With your charm, if you like, your charisma, your presence.

OLIVER. Is that the spoonful of sugar?

SYLVIA. And tonight I don't want you here like that. I've met this man that I am very, very fond of –

OLIVER. She's kicking me out.

SYLVIA. And I have an overwhelming feeling that from now on I'm going to be focusing quite a bit more on him than I am on you.

OLIVER. Fucking kicking me out.

SYLVIA. And I don't think that's a bad thing.

OLIVER. It's over between us.

SYLVIA. For either of us.

Pause.

There. I've said it.

The buzzer rings.

Fuck.

OLIVER. That'll be the future.

SYLVIA. He's early.

OLIVER. I'll be off then.

SYLVIA. Stay. For a quick drink. And then go.

OLIVER. You've made me feel as welcome as a bacon sandwich at a bar mitzvah.

She runs towards the door. Then stops.

SYLVIA. But come tomorrow. To the park. I think...

OLIVER. You think what?

SYLVIA. I think it *is* important. And yes, it's all of those things. A demonstration. A celebration. And a fashion show. But definitely in that order.

OLIVER. The jury's out. Now answer the bloody door.

She runs out of the room. OLIVER *stays there, alone. He becomes pensive, as if trying to remember something. He closes his eyes, and then, almost in a whisper:*

Philip.

1958

A doctor's surgery. Simple. A desk, two chairs, maybe an examination couch. The DOCTOR *and* PHILIP *sit facing each other.*

DOCTOR. When was it that you first experienced sexual attraction to a member of your own sex?

PHILIP. I don't really... I suppose...

DOCTOR. Was it during or after adolescence?

PHILIP. I suppose it was during. Maybe when... maybe when I was thirteen or thereabouts. At school. But of course... well, you understand at that age. I didn't really know. I was frightened, I imagine. So I didn't really. I tried not to think about it. I made myself not think about it.

DOCTOR. Were you interfered with?

PHILIP. I beg your pardon?

DOCTOR. Were you ever interfered with? During your childhood or adolescence. By an adult of your own sex. Were you seduced into any sort of sexual activity by an older male? Either a member of your own family or a teacher or perhaps even a stranger.

PHILIP. No, I wasn't. I didn't...

DOCTOR. You do understand it is absolutely necessary to be truthful in your answering of these questions.

PHILIP. Yes. Of course.

DOCTOR. That unless you answer every one of these questions with absolute honesty and courage you are not only wasting my own time but your own as well. You must attempt to put all inhibitions aside.

PHILIP. I was never seduced. Or interfered with. By anybody.

DOCTOR. So you remember being about thirteen years of age when you first felt sexually attracted to a member of your own sex.

PHILIP. Thereabouts.

DOCTOR. And you indulged in sexual fantasies involving yourself and this boy?

PHILIP. When I was with him I felt... when I was close to him. A strong, overwhelming attraction.

DOCTOR. And your penis would become erect? I mean, there was arousal?

PHILIP. I suppose. I can't really. It was all, sort of connected. Everything was connected.

DOCTOR. 'Connected.' How do you mean, it was 'connected'?

PHILIP. Well, I definitely felt something physical, but it was...

DOCTOR. Did you ever participate in any sort of sexual activity with this boy?

PHILIP. Good God, no. I wasn't... I didn't really know that anyone else... that anyone else had that kind of feeling.

Looking back, I suspect that maybe it was mutual, but at the time.

DOCTOR. Describe to me the fantasies that you had which involved yourself and this boy whom you say you were infatuated with.

PHILIP. I can't really. I suppose we were together. Physically.

DOCTOR. Did you fantasise about anal penetration?

PHILIP. I can't really… Perhaps. Maybe.

DOCTOR. Do you remember if in those fantasies you adopted the sexually passive or the sexually active role?

PHILIP. I honestly can't remember. I do remember wanting to be with him. In a physical sort of way. But I can't remember the details. Maybe I've forced myself to forget them. I'm not sure.

A pause as the DOCTOR *looks over some of the papers he has before him.*

DOCTOR. It says here that you were recently involved in a sexual relationship with a man which persisted over a number of months.

PHILIP. I was, yes.

DOCTOR. I'm assuming that anal intercourse was included in these relations.

PHILIP. Yes. Yes, it was.

DOCTOR. On how many occasions did you have sex with this man?

PHILIP. Well, we were… well, it was over a period of four months.

DOCTOR. And over those four months how many times were you sexually intimate with each other?

PHILIP. Well, it's difficult to say really. Maybe on average two, three times a week.

DOCTOR. And what brought this… this relationship to an end?

PHILIP. I did. I put an end to it.

DOCTOR. In a concerted effort to struggle against this tendency you both shared.

PHILIP. Yes.

DOCTOR. And have you kept in touch with this man? I mean, have you been successful in keeping him out of your life?

PHILIP. Yes.

DOCTOR. And have you banished him from your thoughts?

PHILIP. Sorry?

DOCTOR. Have you been successful in banishing him from your thoughts? Your sexual fantasies.

PHILIP. Yes. I have tried.

DOCTOR. Have you, since the end of this relationship, been involved in any other sexual activity with any other men?

PHILIP. No. No, I haven't.

Pause.

DOCTOR. This is an extreme form of therapy, there is no question about that. Firstly, let me congratulate you on taking the steps you have taken which have brought you here today. I'm sure it has not been easy. From speaking to you briefly this afternoon and from the conversations I have had with Dr Davies, I gather it has been a struggle for you. But fighting this pernicious enemy, this *perversion*, is an essential part in the development of your personality. I'm sure you agree.

PHILIP *says nothing.*

You've brought your belongings.

PHILIP. Yes, I have. A change of clothes. A toothbrush.

DOCTOR. Good. In a few minutes the nurse will take you to your room. The objective is to stay in the room for the length of the treatment. I would suggest till at least tomorrow morning.

PHILIP. All right.

DOCTOR. The room is simple. Spartan. Nothing extraneous. A bed. That is all. There is no window. You may want to brush your teeth beforehand. And get into your pyjamas. Though, of course, we can provide you with something appropriate. Something to wear, I mean.

PHILIP. I've brought my pyjamas.

DOCTOR. Excellent.

Pause.

There are pictures in the room. Publications. We will encourage you to look at them. They are of a pornographic nature and of homosexual content. You will be left alone in the room for approximately an hour. I suggest you spend most of that time looking at these pictures. You will probably be aroused.

Pause.

An hour later, at approximately nine p.m., the nurse will enter the room and inject you with a generous dose of apomorphine. This is a drug that induces vomiting. Around ten to fifteen minutes after the injection you will begin to feel nauseous. You will then be violently sick and may suffer dizziness. Most of the patients undergoing this therapy in the past have asked for a basin, something to vomit into, some sort of receptacle. I have discovered, however, that in order for the treatment to be at its most effective, it is best not to provide you with any such objects. You will vomit in the room and you will have to remain surrounded by your own vomit till the therapy is over in the morning. After the first injection and the first bout of vomiting, it is vital that you try to return to perusing the pornography. A couple of hours later, the nurse will enter again and inject you a second time. This will be repeated three times during the course of the night. And between each injection I would strongly suggest you return to the pornographic images we have provided you with. This will help facilitate the therapy and increase its chances of success.

Pause.

Do you have any questions?

PHILIP. Yes... I... Dr Davies said that in certain cases. Where there is an individual involved.

DOCTOR. Ah, yes. He mentioned it. A few of our patients have asked for the same procedure. I mean, when a particular individual...

PHILIP. Yes.

DOCTOR. You have brought a photograph then. Of this individual.

PHILIP. Yes. Yes, I have.

DOCTOR. Good. Well, it's quite simple, really. You take the photograph with you. Into the room, I mean. Of the individual. You include it. You incorporate it into the treatment. You look at it with the other photographs. This is a common sort of request.

PHILIP. Yes.

Pause.

The thing is, Doctor...

DOCTOR. Yes?

PHILIP. What I need to know is... the other things. The other feelings. I mean, the ones that aren't *exclusively* sexual.

DOCTOR. Yes.

PHILIP. Do they... will they...

There is an awkward pause.

DOCTOR. The nurse will be ready for you now. And I will be seeing you again in the morning.

PHILIP. Yes.

DOCTOR. So there's nothing else then?

PHILIP. No. No, there isn't.

PHILIP *stands up.*

DOCTOR. By the way...

PHILIP. Yes, Doctor?

DOCTOR. Do you mind me asking you what brought you here? What tipped the scales as it were and made you decide to come here? It's an important part of my research.

Pause.

PHILIP. Forgetting.

DOCTOR. Forgetting?

PHILIP. I want an easier life.

DOCTOR. Don't we all?

PHILIP. We do.

Blackout.

2008

The park bench – it is the same one as before. SYLVIA *is sitting on it with* OLIVER. *They have opened a bottle of champagne and are drinking out of flute glasses. In the background there are lots of noises from the Pride party – whistles, shouts, music. The sound of celebration.*

SYLVIA. And every second word is 'gay'. Gay this and gay that. 'You're so gay, it's so gay, they're so gay. Everything's gay.' So there's this one kid and she kind of looks a bit less scary than the rest of them and I just turn around and trying not to sound like her English teacher I say, 'Excuse me'…

OLIVER. Excuse me, miss.

SYLVIA. 'Excuse me, miss, but what exactly does that word mean? I mean, when you use it in that context. Like "That is such a gay song". When you say "That is such a gay song" what exactly does that mean?'

OLIVER. And she says…

SYLVIA. She says it means 'shit'. It means it's shit. The word 'gay' is another word for saying 'shit'.

OLIVER. Gay is shit.

SYLVIA. I mean, the stuff you guys have to put up with. And then like literally the same evening I'm at Jennifer's for dinner.

OLIVER. Why you insist on being her friend is beyond me...

SYLVIA. And she's invited another five or six people including some Spanish guy in pharmaceutics she's crazy about and Millie Wallis, who's had a massive nose job and looks completely different but nobody's allowed to talk about it so we're all pretending that even though her face is *entirely* different we haven't noticed a thing and there's this one guy who's being really quite annoying and pretending to be really liberal but saying something along the lines of, well, it kind of makes sense for the inheritance stuff but they don't really care about the other stuff, whatever that means, I mean, most of them just want to have fun and then Sonya's joining in and saying, and I quote, that 'some of her best friends are gay'...

OLIVER. And most of her exes.

SYLVIA. But it's all kind of gone mad, she's saying, I mean, when's it going to stop and then she's going on about how most of the gay guys she knows are hedonists and spend most of their time in the gym and why should they want to imitate the straights anyway and it's all very much a chorus of 'we all love gay people and aren't they fun and if you ever need advice on wallpaper', but...

OLIVER. But what?

SYLVIA. But I looked at them and they're all...

OLIVER. They're all what?

SYLVIA. I suddenly looked at them and I was listening to what they were saying and they're not bad people, Oliver, I mean, a bit unimaginative, maybe, but not necessarily bad and I'm looking at them and I'm thinking...

OLIVER. You're thinking what?

SYLVIA. Fuck, I don't know how to say this but they *reduce* you.

OLIVER. Reduce me?

SYLVIA. They reduce you, Oliver, to this person who is shallow. Someone who is defined by his body, by what he does with his body and by his taste in things. Clothes, interiors, whatever…

OLIVER. Okay.

SYLVIA. And the thing is you're so much more than that. And somewhere, *somewhere*, you, Oliver, have agreed with them. You've come to an agreement that this is what you are.

OLIVER. I have?

SYLVIA. And I'm thinking of what it was that first made people question things, to push the boundaries, I mean, to stand up for themselves and to really fight and that what they were fighting for can't have been the right to fuck in parks and wear designer clothes…

OLIVER. If you say so…

SYLVIA. After all, the only reason you were in the parks to begin with was because you couldn't be at home. You were kicked out, as it were. In exile.

OLIVER. 'In exile.' I like that.

He pours her some champagne.

Have some more. And now will you kindly step off your fucking soapbox.

PHILIP *enters.*

PHILIP. I could hear you down that hill.

OLIVER. The voice of an actress.

SYLVIA. Was I loud?

PHILIP. Brilliantly so.

SYLVIA. Oh God. I'm a cliché.

Pause.

PHILIP. I brought sandwiches.

SYLVIA. Oliver made some too. Mario's on his way.

OLIVER. What's in them?

PHILIP. Chorizo. Duck. Tapenade.

SYLVIA. I love you guys.

PHILIP. And there's blueberries too.

OLIVER. Yum.

Pause.

SYLVIA. So last night he's talking about kids again.

PHILIP. Who is?

SYLVIA. Mario. 'I've always wanted children,' he says.

OLIVER. He's keen.

SYLVIA. And I think I love this man.

PHILIP. Haven't you just met?

SYLVIA. He writes his own songs. He has a guitar.

OLIVER. That's all she needs to know.

SYLVIA. He never misses an anti-war march. He reads, and reads, and reads.

PHILIP. And?

OLIVER. The signs are all good is what she's saying.

SYLVIA. He's great in bed.

PHILIP. An important thing.

SYLVIA. He makes love to me and I'm thinking... if something should come of this love...

OLIVER. You mean babies?

SYLVIA. If this love is fruitful in that particular way, well then I'm ready for it, God knows I'm ready, and then that's great, I mean, we'll be lucky, it will be a gift. From God. Life. Whatever.

OLIVER. A gift.

PHILIP. She's having kids. I know it.

SYLVIA. And if not, I mean, if it doesn't happen, if it's not meant to happen then that's fine as well. What we have is enough, I mean.

Pause. She's suddenly aware she should leave them alone.

I'm going to... get an ice cream.

OLIVER. An ice cream? But we haven't had lunch.

PHILIP. She wants an ice cream.

OLIVER. I'll come with you.

SYLVIA. With me? How d'you mean, you'll come with me?

OLIVER. I want one too.

SYLVIA. Don't be stupid. Remember our conversation.

OLIVER. Oh, that's right. I'm to stop stalking her.

PHILIP. Stalking her?

OLIVER. Off you go then. You're a free woman.

SYLVIA. At last.

OLIVER. The operation was successful. My arms have been surgically removed from your waist.

SYLVIA. About time.

OLIVER. It's been lovely knowing you.

She starts to move.

SYLVIA. Have some champagne. Finish the champagne.

OLIVER. Okay.

PHILIP. Will do.

She leaves.

OLIVER. Hey.

PHILIP. Hi.

OLIVER. How are you?

PHILIP. Fine. I'm fine.

OLIVER. Good.

A long pause. They look out over the park. They start talking at the same time.

I wasn't –

PHILIP. I hope you don't –

OLIVER. Sorry.

PHILIP. No. What?

OLIVER. After you.

PHILIP. It's fine. You go first.

Pause.

OLIVER. Do you believe in change?

PHILIP. Do I believe in change?

OLIVER. We're really lucky, aren't we?

PHILIP. Lucky.

OLIVER. I mean, think about it. The freedom. What we have.

PHILIP. What freedom?

OLIVER. All these people who were mute. Had been mute for hundreds, thousands of years. For various reasons, I suppose. Poverty, oppression, tradition, hypocrisy, whatever.

PHILIP. Most of the world still is. Mute.

OLIVER. I know. Which makes it all the more...

PHILIP. All the more what?

OLIVER. Important, I think I mean. Not to throw the baby out with the bathwater. For us. If you follow me.

PHILIP. Not really.

OLIVER. I mean, you watch those nature documentaries…

PHILIP. Nature documentaries?

OLIVER. I mean, they're all fucking killing each other, for God's sake. That's all they ever do. Kill each other. And procreate. Inflict terrible pain and kill each other…

PHILIP. Apart from dolphins.

OLIVER. True. They spend all their time swimming with autistic children. But apart from dolphins, they just kill each other. And the only thing, I mean, the only thing that separates us, that makes us different, that makes us *human* is this ability we're discovering, this *thing* we have to instil, to do things with and to give love. And some kind of respect. That's all we fucking have. To listen to each other. To *know* each other.

Pause.

That's what I'm going on about. It's what I was trying to say to you the other day.

PHILIP. When? What?

OLIVER. The night we met. The way you spoke about that woman. The one whose photograph you'd taken. Your ability to put yourself in her shoes. It was genuine.

PHILIP. Oh, that.

OLIVER. And that made me feel hopeful.

Pause.

You still haven't answered my question.

PHILIP. What's that?

OLIVER. Do you believe people change?

PHILIP. That wasn't your question. Your question was do I believe in change. Not do I believe *people* change.

OLIVER. A slight amendment.

PHILIP. *Pourquoi?*

OLIVER. Oh, you know. Us.

PHILIP. What about us?

OLIVER. The thing is…

Pause.

I love you so much. Profoundly.

Pause.

PHILIP. God knows why I came here today.

OLIVER. Because it's mutual?

PHILIP. I don't know what the fuck it is about you. Why the fuck I keep coming back.

OLIVER. I'm irresistible?

PHILIP. Contagious is the word I have in mind.

OLIVER. Charming.

PHILIP. You can be shallow.

OLIVER. Thank you.

PHILIP. Vain.

OLIVER. Lovely.

PHILIP. And you're addicted to sex with strangers.

OLIVER. I've been thinking about that.

PHILIP. But I keep coming back.

OLIVER. Thank you. For the faith, I mean.

PHILIP. The sheer, pig-headed stupidity.

OLIVER. You're very wise in your persistence.

PHILIP. Or completely fucking mad.

OLIVER. Maybe.

PHILIP. After all…

OLIVER. What?

PHILIP. Well, it may not be a long time…

OLIVER. What isn't?

PHILIP. A year and a half, I mean.

OLIVER. Nineteen months. Next Thursday.

PHILIP. Since we've been together.

OLIVER. That's years.

PHILIP. It may not be much, but…

OLIVER. But what?

PHILIP. It's a history of sorts.

OLIVER. Yes.

PHILIP. You and I…

OLIVER. What about us?

PHILIP. We have a history of sorts.

A pause and then OLIVER *is suddenly overwhelmed by an emotion. He pulls back.*

What?

OLIVER. Nothing… I…

PHILIP. What is it?

OLIVER. Nothing. Can I…

PHILIP. Can you what?

OLIVER. Sleep on your floor?

PHILIP. On my floor?

OLIVER. I mean, if things get bad. Money, I mean. It won't be for long...

PHILIP. Explain...

OLIVER. Work. If I'm not earning. For a little while. Until things... I want to work on my book.

PHILIP. I thought you had all these jobs lined up...

OLIVER. They've kind of fallen through.

PHILIP. 'Fallen through'?

OLIVER. Not really me. So times may be hard. For a little while.

PHILIP. Okay. You can sleep over. But the sofa. And then we see. How things go.

OLIVER. That answers my question.

Pause.

PHILIP. And I'm sorry.

OLIVER. What for?

PHILIP. I don't know. If... If I did anything. Ever. To hurt you. To upset you. Whatever. Anything I may have done.

OLIVER. Betrayed me.

PHILIP. Betrayed you?

OLIVER. Yes.

PHILIP. I don't really...

OLIVER. Never mind.

Pause. They look out over the park at the people who surround them. OLIVER *pours* PHILIP *a glass of champagne.*

Have some champagne.

PHILIP. Do you know, I think I will.

They continue to look out.

OLIVER. Have you seen those two? On the bicycle.

PHILIP. They're in love.

OLIVER. The blond one's had his tongue in the other one's ear since we got here.

PHILIP. Yummy.

OLIVER. They're sweet.

PHILIP. And he must be ninety-five.

OLIVER. Who?

PHILIP. The one over there. By the ice-cream van.

OLIVER. I can't see.

PHILIP. Three o'clock. The string vest.

OLIVER. Oh, him. Oh my God.

PHILIP. Ninety-five.

OLIVER. Good on him. A survivor.

PHILIP. Bless him.

OLIVER. If I look like that when I'm ninety-five I'm having a party.

PHILIP. If you look like that when you're ninety-five I'm having you arrested.

SYLVIA *returns but she comes back in her 1950's incarnation. She is wearing her nightie and holding a small suitcase.* OLIVER *and* PHILIP *do not see her and she comes to stand in a pool of light on the other side of the stage from them. It is as if she is sleepwalking.*

SYLVIA. When I next wake, it will be to leave. You will still be sleeping. I will kiss you on your forehead and quietly go, whispering good wishes as I do. We have reached the end of this particular road. I cannot blame you for what you have been. You have been the prisoner of fear. You have only known how to hold onto things and the things you have held onto have died in your hands. Dead ravens in your hands.

The birth pangs will be the pains of you trying to hang onto the way things are. And all I can do is whisper from a distance: it will be all right, it will be all right, it will be all right.

Blackout.

The End.